D1713922

THE SELECTED POEMS OF MIGUEL HERNÁNDEZ

THE SELECTED POEMS OF MIGUEL HERNÁNDEZ

Edited and Translated by Ted Genoways

With Additional Translations by
 Timothy Baland
 Willis Barnstone
 Robert Bly
 John Haines
 Geoffrey Holiday
 Edwin Honig
 Philip Levine
 Gary J. Schmechel
 Don Share
 James Wright

And a Foreword by Robert Bly

The University of Chicago Press
Chicago and London

TED GENOWAYS is the author of *Bullroarer* (2001),
winner of the Samuel French Morse Poetry Prize. He is
also the coeditor of *A Perfect Picture of Hell: Eyewitness
Accounts by Civil War Prisoners from the 12th Iowa* (2001).

The University of Chicago Press, Chicago 60637
The University of Chicago Press, Ltd., London
© 2001 by The University of Chicago
All rights reserved. Published 2001
Printed in the United States of America

10 09 08 07 06 05 04 03 02 01   1 2 3 4 5
ISBN: 0-226-32773-6 (cloth)

"Mi concepto del poema" and the Spanish poems by
Miguel Hernández were published in *Obra Completa*,
Espasa-Calpe. © Vientos del Pueblo, s.l.

Library of Congress Cataloging-in-Publication Data

Hernández, Miguel, 1910–1942.
    [Poems. English & Spanish. Selections]
    The selected poems of Miguel Hernández / edited
    and translated by Ted Genoways with additional
    translations by Timothy Baland . . . [et al.]; and a
    foreword by Robert Bly.
       p.   cm.
    Includes bibliographical references and index.
    ISBN 0–226–32773–6 (cloth : alk. paper)
     1. Hernández, Miguel, 1910–1942—Translations
    into English.   I. Genoways, Ted. II. Title.
    PQ6615.E57 A24 2001
    862′.62—dc21   2001023363

CONTENTS

ILLUSTRATIONS

Hernández shouting his wartime poems to soldiers at the front, 1937 / ii

A photograph of Hernández, originally used as the frontispiece to *El viento del pueblo,* 1937 / x

On leave, Hernández with Josefina, typing up his poems from his handwritten manuscripts in 1937 / xvi

Hernández as a shepherd boy, 1925 / 4

Hernández with soldier friends at the front, 1936 / 102

The only known official photograph of Hernández during his imprisonment, ca. 1940 / 268

The death drawing of Hernández made by one of his fellow inmates, 1942 / 384

Hernández reading his "Elegy" at the dedication of a plaque to Ramón Sijé, Orihuela, 1936 / 386

All illustrations are reprinted here by permission of Ibidem Consulting S.L.

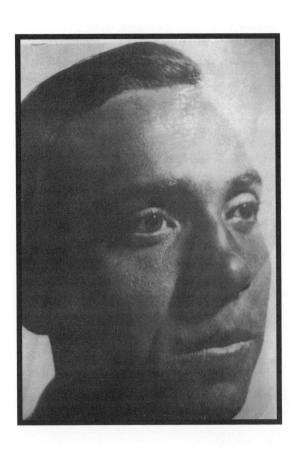

What a victory it is to watch springing forth from our murky thicket of half-commercialized poetry the silver boar of Hernández's words—to see the world of paper part so as to allow the language tusks and shoulders to emerge, shining, pressed forward by his genius. This generous selection of Miguel Hernández's work, arranged, shepherded, and largely translated by Ted Genoways, is an immense gift for which all of us should be grateful. But what we celebrate most is that Hernández's amazing genius appeared at all in this century.

He grew up as a shepherd on a hardscrabble farm, as if Hawthorne had appeared in North Dakota. The canon of the cathedral of Orihuela took an interest in the young shepherd, and as Genoways mentions in his introduction, introduced Hernández to a number of classical Spanish writers, which included Cervantes, Lope de Vega, and Góngora. He fed himself later on the poetry of Jiménez, Lorca, and Neruda; he was given light by his love of Josefina Manresa, and matured by war. But his greatness grew out of the ground of difficult poetry. By that phrase, I am referring to the knot of complicated images that poets in Spain trace back to Góngora, who rejoiced in never saying anything simply.

Góngora, born in 1561, we could say recklessly, and with no slander intended, was the opposite of William Carlos Williams. Williams was a fierce man who disliked all that prevents life from growing, all that keeps a baby from being healthy, and he disliked all in poetry that prevented it from being organic, such as academic glass and parlor cynicism. He wanted each line to be written so that it could be eaten, whether we are poor or rich, college people or high school people. He liked it when a sentence said one thing:

> This is just to say
> I have eaten
> the plums
> that were in
> the icebox. . . .[1]

1. Williams, 372.

He liked it if one could see, so to speak, through the poem as when one
looks down a brightly lit corridor:

> If when my wife is sleeping
> and the baby and Kathleen . . .
> if I in my north room
> danced naked, grotesquely
> before my mirror . . .
> If I admire my arms, my face,
> my shoulders, flanks, buttocks
> against the yellow drawn shades,—
> Who shall say I am not
> the happy genius of my household?[2]

The emotions he was feeling as he wrote the poem were spontaneous
and fresh—not without complication—and yet he wanted each phrase
to be clear, to stand on its own feet, to say one thing and not a lot of
other things. He wanted all the words to lean in one direction like wind
over some blowing grass, so we could admire the shining tips of the
grasses.

Góngora wanted something utterly different. Here are a few of his
lines. He has a poem written to water which begins:

> O bright honor of the liquid element . . .
> Examine how you move and do not lose
> the crystal bridal's wavy rein with which
> you hold in tow the errant moving current.
> It would be wrong for so much beauty to
> be caught, jumbled, and sunken in that ditch,
> seized by the Master of the dripping trident . . .
>
> (TRANSLATED BY WILLIS BARNSTONE)

Góngora wanted every line to say two or three things. He wanted to pull
us back into the natural—geological—confusion that language is. How
does Góngora's longing appear in Hernández?

Miguel Hernández's first book, *Expert in Moons*, published in 1933,
when he was twenty-three years old, contains a group of eight-line po-
ems that puzzled readers. One of these poems begins with the mention
of a narcissus blossom in the first line. The poet Concha Zardoya sug-

2. Williams, 86–87.

gested, as Genoways noted, that the poem was an ode to the moon. We'll
set it down here in Genoways's own English translation:

> White narcissus by obligation.
> Forever facing his reflection, he paints
> with foam, and on the mineral side of the salon,
> an idea of the sea glows, bright and distinct.
> If he does not shear the lathered land,
> he draws lines, with grace, more than ink;
> and at last, his thumb completes the exercise,
> erasing the excesses of his office.

No one could make head or tail out of it. In 1971 Juan Cano Ballesta dis-
covered in manuscript the original titles that Hernández had given to
these poems, titles he withdrew before publication. This poem turned
out to be called "The Barber." So if we now look over the poem again, we
can see in what sense the barber paints foam, the sense in which each
person he shaves resembles a white narcissus at the start, how the mirror
is a bit watery, how the barber draws lines without any ink, and finally
how with his thumb he removes all remaining shaving cream and one
could say gets rid of all his excesses.

In his essay called "Against Abstract Expressionism," Randall Jarrell
comments:

> In the metaphors of painting, as in those of poetry, we are
> awed or dazed to find things superficially so unlike, funda-
> mentally so like; superficially so like, fundamentally so
> unlike.[3]

There you can see the way certain kinds of difficult poetry need to be
praised. In Hernández's next book, *The Unending Lightning*, published
in 1936, he publishes a poem which begins, "You threw me a lemon,"
which I will set down in my own translation. It goes this way:

> You threw me a lemon, oh it was sour,
> with a warm hand, that was so pure
> it never damaged the lemon's architecture.
> I tasted the sourness anyway.

3. Randall Jarrell, *No Other Book: Selected Essays,* ed. Brad Leithauser (New York:
Harperperennial, 1999), 329–30.

With that yellow blow, my blood moved
from a gentle laziness into an anguished
fever, for my blood felt the bite
from a long and firm tip of a breast.

Yet glancing at you and seeing the smile
which that lemon-colored event drew from you,
so far from my dishonorable fierceness,

my blood went to sleep in my shirt,
and the soft and golden breast turned
to a baffling pain with a long beak.

We notice how the lemon seems so different from the warm hand, but a second later that is denied: "I tasted the sourness anyway." So those things that seem unlike are really alike. What he received when the lemon hit his palm was a yellow blow; his real body rose into fever because the round sphere of the lemon felt to his blood like a bite—from a long and firm tip of a breast. That shows how things superficially so unlike can be so fundamentally alike. But to call a breast long, doesn't that distort what a breast is? Randall Jarrell, talking of overly simple lines of abstract expressionism, comes in again and says this:

> One sees in abstract expressionism the terrible esthetic disadvantages of directness and consistency. Perhaps painting can do without the necessity of imitation; can it do without the possibility of distortion?[4]

Now we remember the distortions that El Greco brought into his paintings: one arm of Jesus may be much longer than the other. The painters in the tradition of Bosch rejoiced in distortions. How can we admire Van Gogh without admiring his distortions?

> Yet glancing at you and seeing the smile
> which that lemon-colored event drew from you,
> so far from my dishonorable fierceness,
>
> my blood went to sleep in my shirt,
> and the soft and golden breast turned
> to a baffling pain with a long beak.

4. Jarrell, 331.

Hernández continues to make the poem opaque. How strange to call his fierceness "dishonorable." That makes the line say three or four things at once. In difficult poets, the tip of the plow, so to speak, goes into the ground and hits a big stone. Our poetry longs for that now. How can it be taught in a workshop?

Hernández now reverses direction and says that his blood that had been so anguished—it expected to be wounded—now "went to sleep in my shirt." Perhaps now all the contrary impulses of the language will melt into something creamy, but that's not what happens. Because this is difficult poetry, one has to accept the possibility that

> the soft and golden breast turned
> to a baffling pain with a long beak.

These poems of Hernández are exactly what our poetry needs at this moment. So many poets simply repeat what happened in their childhood, in trying to be accurate. "The necessity of imitation" is driving everyone nuts. Poems are sold to magazines by the yard as dry goods used to be sold in the frontier. Reading American poetry magazines these days is very much like going to the mall; all objects agree to lie down and be themselves and be calm. Hart Crane, on the other hand, said that the ocean was "the great wink of eternity."

It isn't that we don't have difficult poetry, but the only kind of difficult poetry we have, of which Jorie Graham's work is an instance, goes from the intellect to the intellect. When we find our way down through the difficulties of her language we often find ourselves in a mind place that's quite familiar. But Góngora's difficulty, the difficulty of Hernández's exploded octets, lies in the natural, elaborate confusion of emotional language. When we pick our way down through these difficult lines with hints pointing in six directions at once, when we shuck them, so to speak, and get down to what is hidden, it is our emotions that feel the shock. Difficult poetry of the true and vigorous sort does not move from idea to idea, from mind to mind, but moves from the anguished emotions to the intellect and back.

I have said enough now to hint to you how important I think "difficult poetry" has become at this time in the poetry life of the United States, and how essential it is to study the poems in this book.

TED GENOWAYS

Singing I await death,
for there are nightingales that sing
above the muskets
and in the midst of battles.

—MIGUEL HERNÁNDEZ, "WINDS OF THE PEOPLE"

Several years ago, when I was still a graduate student in creative writing
at the University of Virginia, a professor of mine, Douglas Day, men-
tioned to me that he would be lecturing on Spanish poetry to one of his
other classes. He was, and is, a distinguished writer and translator from
the Spanish, so I asked whether I could sit in. Through much of his talk
that following day, he spoke of familiar names, Lorca, Neruda, Vallejo,
but Miguel Hernández was someone I had come across only occasion-
ally—James Wright's translations in *The Collected Poems,* a poem or two
translated by Robert Bly or Timothy Baland in anthologies of twentieth-
century Spanish poets. But, relatively speaking, I knew nothing about his
work. As my professor read, I grew more and more excited by what I was
hearing. Then he quoted a piece of Hernández's famous review of
Neruda's *Residencia en la tierra,* translated by Timothy Baland:

> I am sick of so much pure and minor art. I like the disor-
> dered and chaotic confusion of the Bible, where I see spec-
> tacular events, disasters, misfortunes, worlds turned over,
> and I hear outcries and explosions of blood.
>
> Enough of the coyness and honeyed affectation of poets
> who carry on like candy-making nuns, all daintiness and
> sugared fingertips.[5]

I discovered later that Hernández was twenty-six years old when he
wrote those words, the same age I was as I sat there listening to them. I
could hear myself in him, not only in his bullheaded frustration with
other writers, but in his exacting requirements of his own work. He was
battling to break through toward something new, and hated compla-

---

5. *Selected Poems: Miguel Hernández and Blas de Otero,* 134.

cency in all its forms. It was as though he knew, in some impossible re-
cess of his mind, that his career as a major poet, and indeed his life,
would be over in little more than five years.

I went looking for books by Hernández but could find nothing in the
bookstores. I looked on the Web and found that only Don Share's recent
translations, published in Scotland, were available in print. The last
American publication of a book of poems by Miguel Hernández, a
White Pine Press reprint of the book I had heard my professor read
from, had been printed in 1989—nearly ten years before. So I began
combing the stacks of the university library, collecting poems wherever I
could find them—Willis Barnstone's versions of Hernández from his
book of Spanish sonnets, Philip Levine's translation of "Lullabies of the
Onion" from an old issue of *Antaeus*. But as my collection of poems
grew, so did my dissatisfaction with the gaps.

None of these translations told me much about Hernández beyond
the basic facts of his life: born a goatherd, won the approval of Lorca and
Neruda in Madrid, joined the Loyalist army during the Spanish civil war,
and died of tuberculosis in prison after Franco's Fascist army took con-
trol. There was nothing that revealed his progression as a poet, nothing
to indicate even how one poem related to another chronologically. Soon,
I decided to begin reading the imposing three-volume *Obra completa
(Complete Works)*, published by Espasa-Calpe for the fiftieth anniversary
of Hernández's death in 1992. This edition, prepared by legendary tex-
tual scholar Agustín Sánchez Vidal and José Carlos Rovira with the col-
laboration of Carmen Alemany, was the first definitive edition of
Hernández's work available anywhere. I decided to arrange the best of
the translations I had collected into their proper order, then begin trans-
lating to fill the gaps, writing biographical material to explain the poet's
progress. Somewhere, without thinking, I crossed the line from avid
reader to editor and translator.

I began reading not only the poems, but also the Spanish criticism,
trying to discern the highly regarded poems from the minor works. I
began reading the letters and short prose pieces, then the biographies
and memoirs. I scoured books by Neruda and Vicente Aleixandre for
any mention of Hernández. And one day, as I was poring over a text by
Juan Cano Ballesta, I chanced upon the mention that he was a professor
in the modern language department at my own university. The most
obvious place to look had never occurred to me. An easy walk from
where I had been trying to piece together fragments on my own, sat

Cano, one of a handful of the most highly regarded Hernández scholars in the world. It was the end of the semester, and he was quite busy, but we met a couple of times and exchanged helpful e-mails. He told me stories of meeting Hernández's friends and the exhilaration of finding the notes the young poet had kept that held the answers to the riddle poems of his first book, *Perito en lunas (Expert in Moons)*.

By now, I had assembled too much. I had gathered over 150 poems, many of them minor pieces, and had written countless pages of biographical material. I soon realized that if this was to become a book, I would need to make choices. I would need to select a single translation for poems that had been rendered as many as a half dozen times and I would need to eliminate poems that were not the best of Hernández's work. I found a hint for how to undertake this in an essay by Philip Levine that described Hernández's decision to turn from his early, purely aesthetic poetry toward what Lorca called "another, more generous public minded obsession":

> Well he surely did that, and for a time we who love his poetry were the losers.
>
> Not all the poems from *Viento del Pueblo (Winds of the People)* are as bad as the title poem, but those which strain to take a public position, which serve as rallying cries in the fight against Franco's armies, are.[6]

My guiding principle in selecting which poems were best in the original was to seek those poems which seemed to me most enduring. I don't necessarily agree with Levine's argument that all of Hernández's public poetry was bad, but much of it was written to a specific time and purpose. Reading too much of that now lessens the immediacy of the major work. On the other hand, I think it is important not to attempt to completely aestheticize the work of a popular poet. I have tried to include the best work, but I have also made sure not to exclude any era of his adult career. The entirety of *El rayo que no cesa (The Unending Lightning)* is included, but the purely political poems of *El viento del pueblo (Wind of the People)* and *El hombre acecha (Man Is a Hunter)* have been excluded in favor of the more personal and humane poems detailing Hernández's war experiences. I have included a large portion of Hernández's final masterwork *El cancionero y romancero de ausencias (The Songbook and Ballad-*

6. Philip Levine, "Part of the Problem," *Kenyon Review* 11.4 (Fall 1989): 148.

book of Absences), but in the interest of compression have excluded some of the shorter lyrics, many of which are variations on similar themes.

Selecting the best translations was more difficult. Seamus Heaney once wrote that the key to translation is to recreate "tone" and "tune." I undertook to find those poems which most closely approximated Hernández's original tone and tune, without sacrificing the original meaning. Ironically, some of the most literal translations available are also some of the worst. The syntax of Spanish is entirely different from that of English, but it is more than a simple matter of grammar. Latino poet Alberto Ríos once wrote:

> In English, one says, *I dropped the glass,* should such a thing happen. It is an "I"-centered instance, rugged individualism in its smallest moment. In Spanish, one says, "*Se me calló el vaso,*" which means, "The glass, it fell from me." This is a different world view, a way of accommodating the world, of living with it instead of changing it.[7]

The preponderance of these sorts of reflexive verbs in Spanish puts an unusual burden on a translator trying to reflect this difference of worldview while still making these poems viable in the English language. And this is only the beginning of such challenges. The rhythm is different. The sentence structure is often periodic. As in many romance languages, internal rhymes are pervasive. That adjectives follow nouns in Spanish and carry masculine or feminine endings makes it much easier to achieve end rhymes. Often the translator must decide whether to render rhythm or rhyme, exact meaning or mood. These decisions are especially complex when translating the poems composed in form, but the best translators seem to resolve such conflicts with ease.

Consider the second stanza of the third poem in *The Unending Lightning*. Literally, the stanza reads:

> you have entered my cave, and in it you put
> a network of irritated roots,
> that hold, greedily monopolized
> in their territory, their passions.

Willis Barnstone's translation differs significantly from the literal translation; he renders these lines:

7. Alberto Ríos, "West Real," *Ploughshares* 18.1 (Spring 1992): 4.

you entered in my cave, and in it place
a net of irritated slicing roots
that keep their passions as forbidden fruits
in total greed in this unentered space.

Barnstone changes "territory" to "unentered space," and—more radically—he has altered "that hold, greedily monopolized" to "that keep their passions as forbidden fruits." These are significant changes, but they are consistent with Hernández's language, and the decision was based on completing a rhyme—just as it was when the original was composed. Some might argue that Barnstone's poems are more renderings than pure translations, but I would counter that they convey the music of the original better than any literal translation ever could, and poetry is far more than literal meaning.

In the fifth poem of *The Unending Lightning* the first quatrain literally translates:

Your heart, a frozen orange
with an inside without light of sweet juniper oil
and a porous appearance of gold: an outside
promising chances to the glance.

Robert Bly does not attempt to render the poem in form, but his translation adds punctuation and radically alters sentence structure in the interest of clarity and, therefore, tone. While the above translation is unnecessarily difficult, Bly elegantly renders the stanza thus:

Your heart?—it is a frozen orange,
inside it has juniper oil but no light
and a porous look like gold: an outside
promising risks to the man who looks.

Again, purists might question the insertion of the question mark and dash in the first line, as well as the "it is," but it is clear to me that Bly is trying to approximate the jagged hexameter of the original. "Your heart, a frozen orange" is flat and reads too quickly for the weightiness the poet intends, but in Bly's version the hard caesura of the question mark and dash, followed by the half breath that accompanies "it is" help slow down the line. In contrast, the challenge of the second line is to increase its speed in English. Removing the word "sweet" alters the literal original, but it preserves the tune of the original.

Sometimes the challenge involves translating some untranslatable aspect of the language or the culture. In the final quatrain of his elegy for Ramón Sijé, Hernández wrote:

A las aladas de las rosas
del almendro de nata te requiero
que tenemos que hablar de muchas cosas,
compañero del alma, compañero.

This translates literally as:

To the winged souls of the milky blossoms
of the almond tree, I call you to come,
because we need to speak of many things,
companion of my soul, companion.

Such a literal translation would be adequate, but it fails to convey even a fraction of the heartache in the original. First, the verb *requerir* can mean "to call," but it can also mean "to need." The verb describes a heartsick longing. Second, the word *compañero* is nearly impossible to approximate in English. Though it means literally "companion," it suggests a lifelong friendship like the one shared between Hernández and Sijé, a concept unavailable in a single English word. Thus, Timothy Baland translates the final stanza as:

And I call you to come to the milky
almond blossoms who are souls flying.
I miss you, Ramón. Ramón, we still have
so many things to talk about.

Baland takes the liberty of adding "I miss you" to approximate the longing of *requerir,* and he replaces *compañero* with "Ramón," a gesture of intimacy more familiar to a reader of poetry in English.

The later, free verse poems are less difficult to translate and as Hernández's skills increased, his intimacy and clarity also grew. There may still be occasional variations of turns of phrase from one translation to the next, but the late poems are forcefully and recognizably the voice of the poet, the voice of Miguel Hernández. Though the different translators included here have different interests and strengths, I find that when I take these poems together the vision and power that emerges is unmistakably Hernández.

What a pleasure it has been to assemble this book. I have had the chance to talk in person with Robert Bly about Hernández, to correspond with John Haines and Philip Levine, to speak by phone with Timothy Baland, and exchange e-mails with a new generation of Hernández translators like Don Share, Geoffrey Holiday, and Gary Schmechel. I have taken away a clear vision of what it is that attracts each of these translators, most of them poets themselves, to this poet.

For most, myself included, it is as simple as courage. As a man still in his twenties, Hernández was willing to challenge the poetic establishment of Spain. When his beloved country was threatened by Fascists, he took to the airwaves, shouted his poems to soldiers on their way to the front, and wrote for the magazines they read. When their bodies began to mount in the dark hours of the war, he wrote impassioned elegies to their suffering, and when other poets fled the country to avoid persecution, he refused to leave his family and his countrymen. He was imprisoned and sentenced to death on charges of writing poetry. Though his sentence was commuted to life imprisonment, he was already in the early stages of untreated tuberculosis. Even in the squalor of the prison cells where he would sometimes awaken covered by rats, he continued to write poems on scraps of paper. And when he lay dying on a cot while the pus from his pierced lung oozed on the sheets, he scrawled his final lines on the bare wall.

At a time in our country when arguments about subjects such as "Can Poetry Matter?" take place in air-conditioned lecture halls and conference centers, it is well to remember that there are people in the world for whom poetry is an act of defiance worth risking their lives for. We can debate whether Hernández's poetry mattered in his struggle against oppression, but it would be difficult to argue that his passion didn't matter to the people of Spain.

It was the waning days of the Spanish civil war when Auden wrote in his "In Memory of W. B. Yeats," that "poetry makes nothing happen." The line is often construed as a surrender, a sign that Auden had abandoned hope after the suffering he witnessed in Spain, but the rest of that stanza is rarely quoted:

. . . poetry makes nothing happen: it survives
In the valley of its saying where executives
Would never want to tamper; it flows south
From ranches of isolation and the busy griefs,

Raw towns that we believe and die in; it survives,
A way of happening, a mouth.[8]

Thus, for Auden, poetry may not have been a means of ending suffering, but it resides in a space rarely invaded by dictators and thus it survives to provide a record. Even in death, it is a mouth. Though Hernández's life was cut tragically short, his brief years of song survive, and the power of his words resounds like the sad melodies of his beloved nightingales. Long after the muskets and cannon fire, we hear his singular voice.

8. W. H. Auden, *Selected Poems*, ed. Edward Mendelson (New York: Vintage Books, 1979), 82.

The Spanish text of this volume has been prepared from the three-volume *Obra completa,* edited by Agustín Sánchez Vidal and José Carlos Rovira with the collaboration of Carmen Alemany and published by Espasa-Calpe in 1992. Much of the ordering of these poems would have been impossible without this extended revision of Hernández's work. Thanks to the editors and publishers of this landmark volume for permission to use their work to set a corollary benchmark in English.

Additional thanks are due all the contributing translators, all of whom allowed their work to be included for little or nothing. Among these, specials thanks go to Robert Bly for contributing his fine foreword, to Don Share for early encouragement and guidance, and Geoffrey Holiday for his enthusiasm in the late stages of this project. Thanks to Juan Cano Ballesta for taking the time to work with me on some of the difficult intricacies of the *octavas* in *Perito en lunas;* to Charles Wright for encouraging me to pursue this project and suggesting possible places to send it; to Virgil Suarez for his unwavering and vocal belief that a book like this was needed; to Enrico Santí for his suggestions concerning my translation of Octavio Paz's "Recoged esa voz," which closes this volume.

Most of all, I must thank: my father, who insisted that I learn Spanish in the first place, then badgered me until I began to consider doing serious translations; Randy Petilos, my editor at the University of Chicago Press, who had the foresight to ask to see this project and the fortitude to see it through; and my family, especially my wife Mary Anne, for weathering several years of work on this book. To all of you, my deepest thanks. Without you, truly, this would never have happened.

A number of these translations originally appeared in earlier publications:

John Haines's translation of "Love climbed between us" appeared as a limited edition chapbook under the title *El Amor Ascendía* (Ox Head Press, 1967); courtesy of John Haines.

Translations by Robert Bly, James Wright, Timothy Baland, and Hardie St. Martin appeared in *Selected Poems: Blas de Otero and Miguel Hernández,* ed. Timothy Baland and Hardie St. Martin (Beacon Press, 1972); courtesy of Robert Bly.

Philip Levine's translation of "Lullabies of the Onion" appeared originally in *Antaeus* 15 (Autumn 1974): 32–34, and was reprinted in *Roots and Wings: Poetry from Spain, 1900–1975,* ed. Hardie St. Martin (Harper & Row, 1976); courtesy of Philip Levine.

Translations by Michael Smith appeared in *The Unceasing Lightning* (Dedalus Press, 1986); courtesy of Dedalus Press, Ireland.

Translations by Edwin Honig appeared in *The Unending Lightning: The Selected Poems of Miguel Hernández* (Sheep Meadow Press, 1990); courtesy of Sheep Meadow Press.

Translations by Willis Barnstone appeared in *Six Masters of the Spanish Sonnet* (Southern Illinois University Press, 1996); courtesy of Southern Illinois University Press.

Translations by Don Share appeared in *I Have Lots of Heart* (Bloodaxe Books, 1997); courtesy of Bloodaxe Books, Scotland.

Translations by Ted Genoways of "The Letter" and "Song of the Anti-aircraft Gunner" appeared in *Virginia Quarterly Review* 75.4 (Autumn 1999): 680–684; "To My Son" and Section 25 of *The Unending Lightning* (as "Sonnet") appeared in *Quarterly West* 49 (Fall-Winter 1999); Section 18 of *The Unending Lightning* (as "Perhaps") appeared in *Partisan Review* 66.4 (Fall 1999): 608; "Recoged esa voz" © 1942 by Octavio Paz, reprinted by permission of Marie José Paz.

THE SELECTED POEMS OF MIGUEL HERNÁNDEZ

¿Qué es el poema? Una bella mentira fingida. Una verdad insinuada. Sólo insinuándola, no parece una verdad mentira. Una verdad tan preciosa y recóndita como la de la mina. Se necesita ser minero de poemas para ver en sus etiopías de sombras sus indias de luces. Una verdad de la sal en situación azul y cantora. ¿Quién ve la marina verdad blanca? Nadie. Sin embargo existe, late, se alude en el color lunado de la espuma en bulto. El mar evidente, ¿sería tan bello como en su sigilo si se evidenciara de repente? Su mayor hermosura reside en su recato. El poema no puede presentársenos Venus o desnudo. Los poemas desnudos so la anatomía de los poetas. ¿Y habrá algo más horrible que un esqueleto? Guardad, poetas, el secreto del poema: esfinge. Que sepan arrancárselo como una corteza. ¡Oh, la naranja: qué delicioso secreto bajo un ámbito a lo mundo! Salvo en el caso de la poesía profética en que todo ha de ser claridad—porque no se trata de ilustrar sensaciones, de solear cerebros con el relámpago de la imagen de la talla, sino de propagar emociones, de avivar vidas—, guardáos, poetas, de dar frutos sin piel, mares sin sal. Con el poema debiera suceder lo que con el Santísimo Sacramento . . . ¿Cuándo dirá el poeta con el poema incorporado a sus dedos, como dice el cura con la hostia: «Aquí está DIOS» y lo creeremos?

MIGUEL HERNÁNDEZ
(ORIHUELA, CERCA 1933)

What is a poem? A beautiful affected lie. An insinuated truth. Only by insinuating it will a truth not appear a lie. A truth as precious and hidden as anything from a mine. One needs to be a miner of poems to see in its Ethiopias of darkness its Indias of light. A salt-wizened truth situated between blue and singing. Who sees that the sea in truth is white? Nobody. Nevertheless it exists, it flutters, it alludes in its sculpted spume to the color of the crescent moon. The clear sea—would it be as beautiful as its secret if it were suddenly clarified? Its greater beauty lies in its secrecy. The poem cannot present itself to us as either Venus or naked. Naked poems have only the anatomy of poems. And who could make something more horrible than a bare skeleton? Guard, poets, the secret of the poem: a sphinx. Let them learn to tear it away like bark from a tree. Oh, like the orange: what a delicious secret under its planetary circumference! Except in the case of prophetic poetry for which clarity is essential—because it does not try to illustrate sensations, or dazzle the mind with the lightning flash of a sculpted image, but rather to propagate emotions, to enliven lives—guard yourselves, poets, against fruits without skins, seas without salt. The poem has to work as with the Holy Sacrament. . . . When will the poet come with a poem in his fingers, like a priest with the host, saying "Here is GOD" and we will believe it?

MIGUEL HERNÁNDEZ
(ORIHUELA, CIRCA 1933)

TED GENOWAYS

THE EARLY POEMS: 1923–1936

The Shepherd Poet

Miguel Hernández was born October 30, 1910, to a poor goatherding family in the village of Orihuela, in the province of Alicante, Spain. The full extent of his formal education is unknown—various biographers estimate from two to seven years of schooling. What is certain is that his time at the Jesuit Colegio de Santo Domingo was cut short by his father's disapproval. Miguel Hernández Sánchez did not feel that his bright son should be allowed to progress to the university while his other son was left to tend the family herd. In 1926, at age fifteen, Hernández was forced to leave the Colegio and join his father and brother herding goats and sheep in the hills surrounding Orihuela. It was the last formal education he would ever receive.

Hernández continued to read voraciously, however, on his own. Seeing his young parishioner's interest in literature, Don Luis Almarcha, canon of the cathedral of Orihuela, directed Hernández to classical Spanish literature, such as Cervantes, Lope de Vega, Góngora, and Garcilaso, as well as the writings of St. John of the Cross and Fray Luis de Léon's translation of Virgil. His readings led to contemporary Spanish writers. His favorite was Juan Ramón Jiménez, but he also devoured Antonio Machado, Jorge Guillén, Gabriel y Galán, Rubén Darío, and translations of Valéry and Verlaine. Soon he also discovered the lyrical novels of Gabriel Miró, whom Hernández later credited as his chief inspiration and influence.

Inevitably, he began to try his own hand at poetry, writing mostly brief lyrics on the subjects familiar to him. One of his earliest surviving pieces, entitled "Pastoril" ("Pastoral"), reveals both his tentative steps into verse and the overwhelming confinement he felt as a young intellectual trapped in his life as a goatherd:

> Crouching, I milk
> a goat and a dream.
>
> Glug, glug, glug,
> goes the milk falling
> in the pail. The sky-blue
> tissue is going to dawn.

Glug, glug, glug. The spume rises
and exhales
the finest sea-fog.

(I milk another goat, faster.)

Crouching, I milk
a goat and a dream.[1]

Unfortunately, for the young poet, these daydreams and his constant reading sometimes led to moments of inattention. His father beat him often for losing sheep from the herd or if he caught his son reading late into the night when he should have been resting for the next day's work.

Undeterred, Hernández continued to read and write poems until, at eighteen, he became a member of an informal group of aspiring writers. The group consisted of Carlos and Efrén Fenoll, who hosted the meetings in the back room of their family bakery, and Justino and José Gutiérrez—writing poems under their pen names Ramón and Gabriel Sijé. Ramón, without question, became the single most important influence on the early poetry of Miguel Hernández.

Though he was two years younger, Sijé was considerably more worldly—he was a law student, had already published a number of critical reviews, and (most important to Hernández) was allied with the extreme reformist Catholics, who shared Gabriel Miró's desire for political and religious change in Orihuela. Sijé's political stock would continue to rise as he became editor of the short-lived but influential *Voluntúd* (March-July 1930) and subsequently *El gallo crisis* (1934–1935).

Hernández published his poetry in *Voluntúd* and the weekly *El pueblo de Orihuela*. Before long his poems began to appear in larger, more regional journals, and soon he attained a small reputation as "the shepherd poet of Orihuela." Though the attention was flattering, Hernández feared being forever categorized as a simple poet, respected only in the rural provinces of Spain. Against the advice of Sijé and the other members of his Orihuelan writing group, in December 1931 Miguel Hernández gathered his meager belongings and set out to conquer the literary center of Madrid.

1. Hernández, *Obra completa*, 1: 118. All translations are mine unless indicated otherwise.

The First Trip to Madrid

The six months between December 1931 and May 1932 were difficult for Hernández. The thriving literary community he had expected—though it undoubtedly existed—did not open its doors to him. Here was an unknown goatherd, dismissed without notice. Worse still, he was often confused and overwhelmed by the constant bustle of the city. He wrote:

> I saw myself small and soft on the sidewalks
> of a city resplendent with chandeliers.
> Difficult canyons of stairs,
> quiet cataracts of elevators—
> what an impression of emptiness!—
> occupying the place of my flowers,
> the murmuring of my winds and my river.[2]

Perhaps, it was this disillusionment that led Hernández to become enamored of the neo-Gongorine movement; in retreat from the crush of city life, his poems delved into the extreme imagism and idealized landscapes he had admired in Góngora as a youth. Or perhaps, the lingering members of neo-Gongorism were the only people in Madrid to whom Hernández felt any outsider kinship. It is also possible, as Geraldine Cleary Nichols posits, that Hernández did not undergo his shift toward the deeper, more enigmatic *décimas* and *octavas* (the intricately rhymed ten- and eight-line poems of this period) until "after the chastened 'shepherd poet' returned from Madrid."[3] Certainly, it seems unlikely that Hernández would have undertaken such an extended project as *Perito en lunas* (*Expert in Moons*) without the approval of Ramón Sijé. The months from May to December 1932, back in the safety of Orihuela, were spent composing and reworking these poems.

In January 1933, *Expert in Moons* was published with the financial backing of friend José Martínez Arenas and Hernández's first literary

---

2. "El silbo de afirmación en la aldea" ("The whistle of affirmation in the city"), Hernández, *Obra completa*, 1: 373.

3. Nichols, 20. The single best source of English analysis of Miguel Hernández's poetry remains *Miguel Hernández*, by Geraldine Cleary Nichols. Nichols blends well-researched and documented biographical material with careful critical analysis. Her translations, though sometimes unnecessarily literal, also provide serviceable renderings of excerpts from poems not included here. Any study of Hernández's poetry, by a speaker of English, should begin with this excellent work.

mentor, Don Luis Almarcha. In support of the book, Hernández sent copies to all the major Spanish poets of the day and went with Sijé on a tour of coffee houses and literary clubs around Alicante. Sijé would lecture first, using his fiery oratory and strong command of Spanish literature to draw a direct line from Góngora to Hernández, proclaiming his friend the heir to the grand Spanish tradition. After this extended introduction, Hernández would take the podium and read his poems. Not surprisingly, audiences generally did not share Sijé's enthusiasm.

Part of the problem was that this first edition of *Expert in Moons* carried no titles. Without them, many of these poems became riddles for readers and reviewers to unlock, most of which went unexplained for years. Nichols points out that Concha Zardoya believed that *octava* XIV—describing a "white narcissus" who "[a]lways facing his own image . . . paints foam"—was an ode to the moon.[4] In 1971, when Juan Cano Ballesta published in *La poesía de Miguel Hernández* the manuscript titles Hernández himself had withheld, poem XIV was revealed to be "Barbero" ("The Barber"). Such a shift in interpretation is inestimable. Because these titles have revolutionized our understanding of *Expert in Moons,* and because Cano's source is redoubtable (notes Hernández had dictated to a friend in Orihuela who wished to teach the book),[5] they are in every case included in this translation.

Even with their titles, the extreme compression of these early poems and the overwhelming demands of their rhyme schemes often sink even the finest of Hernández's *octavas* into obscurity. Perhaps the best-known example of the complex syntax of these poems is in "El Toro" ("The Bull"); two lines in the original read:

> Por el arco, contra los picadores,
> del cuerno, flecha, a dispararme parto.

Nichols points out the difficulty of this sentence when she says, "This means: I depart like an arrow to shoot myself through the bow of [formed by] the horns at the picadors."[6] Perhaps, but clearly this is not poetry. Yet, a literal translation would be nonsensical:

> Through the bow, at the picadors,
> of the horn, arrow, to fire myself I begin.

4. Ibid., 53.
5. Cano Ballesta, 61.
6. Nichols, 29.

For his *Introduction to Modern Spanish Literature,* published in 1968, Kessel Schwartz translated these lines as:

> Through the arch, against the picadors
> I go like an arrow of horns.[7]

This is certainly one option. However, translating *arco* as "arch" and removing the verb *dispararme,* a reflexive form that precludes translation as anything other than "fire myself," eliminates some of the complexity of Hernández's poem. In the original, the bull is both the bow and the arrow, and trusting the syntax, the horns form the bow and the body of the bull forms the arrow. I have translated the lines:

> From the bow of my horns, I fire
> my body like an arrow at the picadors.

That the resulting image is slightly counterintuitive (as opposed to Schwartz's more logical "arrow of horns") is a characteristic of the original poem. Thus, I have chosen to render faithfully this and other early poems so that discussion is possible as to whether such imagery is a harbinger of future dislocations in Hernández's poems or simply a weakness of his early verse. Critics at the time—perhaps confused, perhaps aloof—were almost unanimously silent.

In mid-April 1933, frustrated by what he considered the unaccountable dismissal of *Expert in Moons,* Hernández wrote to Federico García Lorca, one of the poets whom he had met in Madrid, pouring his frustration and his passion into his letter:

> You know well that there are things difficult to understand in this book of mine and that it is a book of resuscitated, renovated forms, that it is a first book and hidden in its guts is more personality, more courage, more *cojones*—in spite of its false air of Góngora—than in all those of almost all the consecrated poets . . .

He concludes:

> Federico: I don't want you to pity me; I want you to understand me.
> Here, in my orchard, in my sheep pen, I await your favorable reply, and soon, or simply a reply; here, plastered up

7. Schwartz, 264.

like a poster on this mudwall, behind which poor parents
live, with so many children and so little house, and because
of this the children do not see the origins of their fabrica-
tion, the beginning of their brothers, and they leave down
the narrow alley to reacquaint themselves with the most ex-
alted nights.[8]

Lorca seems to have taken pity on the young poet, perhaps admiring
his intensity, but also feeling the need to chide him gently for overstating
the accomplishments of his own poems:[9]

My dear poet:

I haven't forgotten you. But I'm doing a good bit of living
and my pen keeps slipping out of my hand.

I think about you often because I know you're suffering in
that circle of literary pigs, and it hurts me to see your energy, so
full of sunlight, fenced in and throwing itself against the walls.

But you'll learn that way. You'll learn to keep a grip on
yourself in that fierce training life is putting you through.
Your book stands deep in silence, like all first books, like my
first, which had so much delight and strength. Write, read,
study, FIGHT! Don't be vain about your work. Your book is
strong, it has many interesting things, and to eyes that can
see makes clear *the passion of man,* but it doesn't, as you
say, have more *cojones* than those of the most established
poets.[10] Take it easy. Europe's most beautiful poetry is being
written in Spain today. But, at the same time, people are not
fair. *Expert in Moons* doesn't deserve that stupid silence. No.

8. Hernández, *Obra completa,* 3: 2307.

9. This translation by Hardie St. Martin appears in Hernández and de Otero, *Selected
Poems,* 36–37, with the editorial note that "[t]he letter was copied by Concha Zardoya from
the original in the house of Josefina Manresa, the widow of Miguel Hernández. It was pub-
lished first in *Bulletin hispanique,* July-September 1958." It should be noted that the letter
was published in that issue by Marie Laffranque.

10. St. Martin's original translation of this clause reads, "although, as you say, it
doesn't have any more *cojones* than those of the most established poets," 36. St. Martin's
translation was made from Lorca's letter without benefit of the letter by Hernández. Thus it
was an understandable error to misplace the phrase, "as you say"; after comparing Hernán-
dez's letter, however, we must assume that Lorca is refuting Hernández's claim that *Expert
in Moons* contains "more personality, more courage, more *cojones* . . . than in all those of
almost all the consecrated poets."

It deserves the attention and encouragement and love of good people. You have that and will go on having it because you have the blood of a poet and even when you protest in your letter you show, in the middle of savage things (that I like), the gentleness of your heart, that is so full of pain and light.

I wish you'd get rid of your obsession, that mood of the misunderstood poet, for another more generous, public-minded obsession. Write to me. I want to talk to some friends and see if they'll take an interest in *Expert in Moons.*

Books of poetry, my dear Miguel, catch on very slowly.

I know perfectly well what you are like and I send you my embrace like a brother, full of affection and friendship.

(Write to me)

—Federico

Lorca's advice seems to have been heeded. Over the remainder of 1933 and into 1934, Hernández embarked on an ambitious period of experimentation, where almost without exception he struggled to abandon the contorted syntax and obscurity of *Expert in Moons* for something "more generous." By early 1934, his poetry had found its new form in the sonnet, and Hernández had found a new subject in his growing passion for a girl named Josefina Manresa whom he had seen working in the village sewing shop. She was the daughter of a member of the notorious Guardia Civil, but this made no difference to Hernández.

Soon they were in love and he was writing furious sonnets for a planned work, *El silbo vulnerado (The Wounded Whistle).* The title derives from Hernández's mixed feelings of nostalgia and humility about his "crude life,"[11] as he calls it in one poem. As a goatherd he learned a series of whistles to send commands to the flock and the dogs that helped herd them. To escape the disapproving eyes of Josefina's father, Hernández taught these whistles to his new love and would signal her when he had arrived outside the walls of the Guardia compound. The love-wracked poems of that time transform these realities into metaphoric explorations. The sonnet from which the title is drawn reads:

Pain makes one whistle, I have witnessed it,
when he feels pain, deeply wounding pain,

11. "[M]i vida cruda," Hernández, *Obra completa,* 1: 480.

pain of harsh helplessness,
pain of love-sick loneliness.

What loving nightingale—pallid, fervent
and afflicted—has not lanced
some heart from the illustrious loneliness of its nest
with its love-struck wounded whistle?

What exquisite turtledove can resist,
faced with kind but crude silence,
expressing its pity as a widow?

I whistle in my loneliness, sad bird,
with such an inexhaustible devotion
that the mountains follow me always mute.[12]

Though still a journeyman work, this poem reflects the surprising leaps Hernández's poetry was beginning to make. His confidence reflected these changes, and in May 1934—less than two years after he had returned defeated from Madrid—he decided again to try to make his name in the capital city.

The Second Trip to Madrid

Miguel Hernández's second excursion to Madrid could not have been more different from his first. With the advantage of added age and maturity, he arrived with copies of *Expert in Moons,* the manuscript of his miracle play, and the first sonnets of his new poetry manuscript. Almost immediately upon his arrival, José Bergamín agreed to publish the entirety of Hernández's play *Quien te ha visto y quien te ve (Who Has Seen You and Sees You Still)* in his influential reformist Catholic journal, *Cruz y raya.*

With this acclaim and *Expert in Moons* as entrée, Hernández renewed his friendship with Federico García Lorca and began to meet all the major poets of Spain: Rafael Alberti, Manuel Altolaguirre, and Luis Cernuda. Even amid the excitement, he still felt some of the confusion and homesickness he had experienced two years before. Now the feelings

12. Ibid., 485.

were strengthened by his longing for Josefina. In the early months of his time in Madrid, he wrote to her twice a week, often complaining of the sheer bustle of the city:

> I go about like a sleepwalker, sadly, in and out of these streets filled with smoke and streetcars, so different from those hushed and happy streets of our land. What I regret most is not to see the processions with you, not to give you candies with my lips and kisses with my imagination. . . . Maybe I should move to another place. Where I am is very expensive. I pay ten *reales* a day just for bed, laundry and breakfast. . . . Besides, the apartment under mine is an academy of dancers and cabaret singers and they don't let me get anything done with their piano racket, songs and stamping.[13]

Worse still, Hernández was trapped in that tiny apartment because he simply couldn't afford more. In fact, when Vicente Aleixandre published *La destrucción o el amor (Destruction or Love),* Hernández wrote him a letter to say that he had seen the book in a local shop and admired it but didn't have the money to buy it. Aleixandre wrote back, inviting Hernández to his home. He gave him a copy of *Destruction or Love,* and the two began a life-long friendship.

Around this same time, Hernández made an even more influential friend in Pablo Neruda, who was then Chile's consul to Spain. In his *Confieso que he vivido: Memorias (Memoirs),* he wrote, "The young poet Miguel Hernández was one of Federico's and Alberti's friends. I met him when he came up, in espadrilles and the typical corduroy trousers peasants wear, from his native Orihuela."[14] Neruda was immediately taken with what he perceived as Hernández's "aura of earthiness" with "a face like a clod of earth or a potato that has just been pulled up from among the roots and still has its subterranean freshness."[15] As an example of his unpretentious, country simplicity, Neruda remembered, in an interview with Robert Bly in 1966, one particular night in 1934 when the two men were walking together in Madrid:

> I said to him that I had never heard a nightingale, because no nightingales exist in my country. You see, it is too

---

13. Zardoya, 20, quoted in and translated by Barnstone, 265.
14. Neruda, 117, translated by Hardie St. Martin.
15. Ibid.

cold for nightingales in my country; and then he said, "Oh, you've never heard . . ." and he climbed up a tree and he whistled like a nightingale from very high up. Then he climbed down and ran to another tree and climbed up and made another whistle like a nightingale, a different one.[16]

And in his memoirs, Neruda recalled:

He would tell me how exciting it was to put your ear against the belly of a sleeping she-goat. You could hear the milk coursing down to the udders, a secret sound no one but that poet of goats has been able to listen to.[17]

The admiration was mutual. Hernández began to read with the same ferocity he had felt as a youth, but now he was reading the poems of his friends Neruda and Aleixandre. In these poets, Hernández saw ways to escape the poetic confinement Lorca had warned him against. Not only were these poets writing in free verse and without rhyme, but they used a freer, more associative style of writing, and Neruda was calling for poetry that dared to examine the ordinary, even the impure. Neruda wrote, "He was living and writing in my house. My American poetry, with other horizons and plains, had its impact and gradually made changes in him."[18]

In order to support Hernández, Neruda tried to use his influence as Chilean consul to secure Miguel a position in the Spanish government:

At last a viscount, a high official in the Ministry of Foreign Relations, took an interest in his case and replied that yes, he was all for it, he had read Miguel's poems, admired them, and Miguel just had to indicate what position he preferred and he would be given the appointment.

I was jubilant and said: "Miguel Hernández, your future is all set, at last. The viscount has a job for you. You'll be a high-ranking employee. Tell what kind of work you want, and your appointment will go through."

Miguel gave it some thought. His face, with its deep, premature lines, clouded up with anxiety. Hours went by and it

16. Hernández and de Otero, *Selected Poems*, 136.
17. Neruda, 117, translated by St. Martin.
18. Ibid.

was not until late in the afternoon that he gave me his answer. With the radiant look of someone who has found the solution to his whole life, he said to me: "Could the viscount put me in charge of a flock of goats somewhere near Madrid?"[19]

Instead Hernández took a job from his friend José María de Cossío, an editor at the prestigious publishing house Espasa-Calpe, writing entries on famous bullfighters for the encyclopedia *Los toros (The Bullfights)*. Shortly after starting work, Hernández wrote a friend, "I earn very little: forty *duros* monthly, but I am in the atmosphere that I need in these times of mine."[20] The "atmosphere" he spoke of consisted of frequent conversations with people he had previously only read or written letters to. He had the support and companionship of Lorca and Altolaguirre, as well as increasingly close friendships with Vicente Aleixandre and Neruda, who by now was almost a father figure in Miguel's life.

In late 1935, Neruda published the first issue of his groundbreaking literary magazine, *Caballo verde para la poesía (The Green Horse of Poetry)*. He spelled out his ideas for this new poetry in the prologue to the inaugural issue:

> Let the poetry that we seek be thus, worn as if with acid by the tasks of the hand, impregnated with sweat and fumes, smelling of urine and of lilies, splattered with the various excesses that are committed within and without the law. A poetry as impure as a dress, as a body, with food stains, and shameful positions, with wrinkles.[21]

Neruda's ideas about what constitutes art had wide-ranging implications for Hernández, not only in his poetry, but in every phase of his life. Josefina did not share her *novio*'s increasingly free spirit, and on their occasional visits Hernández grew increasingly upset over her Catholic beliefs, especially when it came to what María de Gracia Ifach called "her exaggerated chastity bordering on prudishness."[22] Soon, he wrote her:

> It seems to me that I am not the man you need. . . . I have my life here in Madrid, it would be impossible for me to live

19. Ibid., 117–118.
20. Hernández, *Obra completa*, 3: 2345.
21. Quoted in and translated by Nichols, 23.
22. Quoted in and translated by ibid., 22.

in Orihuela now; [here] I have friends who comprehend me perfectly, there no one understands me and no one cares about anything I do.[23]

After that, for almost a year, they corresponded rarely and only in brief, cordial letters. Josefina wasn't the only one in Orihuela upset with the changes Hernández was undergoing. Ramón Sijé had come across the first issue of *Caballo verde* and was scandalized by his friend's turn toward the new surrealism in "Vecino de la muerte" ("Death's Neighbor") and horrified by the poem "Mi sangre es un camino" ("My Blood Is a Road"). Sijé sent a venomous letter on November 29, 1935:

It is terrible not to have sent me *Caballo verde*. . . . Although of course *Caballo verde* shouldn't interest me much. There is no trace in it of poetic fury, nor polemical fury. Impure and sectarian horse. . . . The one who is suffering a great deal is you, Miguel. Someday I will blame *someone* for your present sufferings. A terrible and cruel transformation. The reading of your poem "My Blood is a Road" tells me everything. Truly, a road of melancholy horses. But not the road of a man, not the road of human dignity. Nerudism (how disgusting! Pablo and the forest, a narcissistic and subhuman ritual of groins, of soft little hairs in forbidden parts and of forbidden horses!); Aleixandrism, Albertism.[24]

Surely, Hernández must have been filled with rage upon receiving this letter, but before he could reply, his anger was turned to sorrow. This letter would be their last communication.

On Christmas Eve 1935, after an exhausting effort to finish an exam on romanticism, Sijé died suddenly at the age of only twenty-three. Miguel found out through Vicente Aleixandre, who had read the obituary in the newspaper. Heartbroken, Hernández wrote to Sijé's parents: "My pain is as large as yours. I don't know what to say to console you, because I cannot find the words."[25] But he was already at work on his famous and tortured terza rima elegy for Sijé, and a companion poem for Sijé's fiancée.

23. Ibid.
24. Zardoya, 23–24, quoted in and translated by Nichols, 24.
25. Hernández, *Obra completa,* 1: 2365.

His sequence of sonnets complete and now retitled *El rayo que no cesa (The Unending Lightning)*, Hernández would never be able to send Sijé a copy of the printed book scheduled to appear in February 1936. He was able, however, to quickly arrange to have his elegy included as the penultimate poem in his first full-length book. It would be the book that would establish Hernández as a major figure among Spanish poets, and soon it would make him a target amid the growing political unrest in his beloved Spain.

PERITO EN LUNAS
(1933)

EXPERT IN MOONS

(1933)

3

[TORO]

> ¡A la gloria, a la gloria toreadores!
> La hora es de mi luna menos cuarto.
> Émulos imprudentes del lagarto,
> magnificáos el lomo de colores.
> Por el arco, contra los picadores,
> del cuerno, flecha, a dispararme parto.
> ¡A la gloria, si yo antes no os ancoro
> —golfo de arena—, en mis bigotes de oro!

3

[THE BULL]

To your glory, go to your glory, bullfighters!
It is the hour of my moon, less a quarter.
Unwise rivals of the lizard,
they make the dirt magnificent with color.
From the bow of my horns, I fire
my body like an arrow at the picadors.
What glory, if first they are not anchored—
on this sand-gulf—by my mustache's golden handlebars!

TED GENOWAYS

4

[*TORERO*]

Por el lugar mejor de tu persona,
donde capullo tórnase la seda,
fiel de tu peso alternativo queda,
y de liras el alma te corona.
¡Ya te lunaste! Y cuanto más se econa,
más. Y más te hace eje de la rueda
de arena, que desprecia mientras junta
todo tu oro desde punta a punta.

4

[THE BULLFIGHTER]

Through the better part of your body,
where silkworms spin gossamer,
the soul remains faithful to your other power
and crowns you with lyres and poetry.
Now you are stained! It makes you angry;
and more, it makes you axis and arbor
of the sandy wheel that scorns even as it joins
all your gold from horn to horn.

TED GENOWAYS

[EL BARBERO]

Blanco narciso por obligación.
Frente a su imagen siempre, espumas pinta,
y en el mineral lado de salón
una idea de mar fulga distinta.
Si no equileo en campo de jabón,
hace rayas, con gracia, mas sin tinta;
y al fin, con el pulgar en ejercicio,
lo que le sobra anula de oficio.

14

[THE BARBER]

White narcissus by obligation.
Forever facing his reflection, he paints
with foam, and on the mineral side of the salon,
an idea of the sea glows, bright and distinct.
If he does not shear the lathered land,
he draws lines, with grace, more than ink;
and at last, his thumb completes the exercise,
erasing the excesses of his office.

TED GENOWAYS

[HORNO Y LUNA]

Hay un constante estío de ceniza
para curtir la luna de la era,
más que aquélla caliente que aquél ira,
y más, si menos, oro, duradera.
Una imposible y otra alcanzadiza,
¿hacia cuál de las dos haré carrera?
Oh tú, perito en lunas; que yo sepa
qué luna es de mejor sabor y cepa.

35

[OVEN AND MOON]

There is an unending summer of ash
that hard-bakes the threshing-floor moon,
more like slow fire than a sudden flash,
and, if of less duration, then more golden.
One impossible, the other within reach,
toward which of the two does my course run?
Oh you, expert in moons; would that I knew,
for pedigree and flavor, which moon to choose.

TED GENOWAYS

[*FUNERARIO Y CEMENTERIO*]

Final modisto de cristal y pino;
a la medida de una rosa misma
hazme de aquél un traje, que en un prisma,
¿no? se ahogue, no, en un diamante fino.
Patio de vecindad menos vecino,
del que al fin pesa más y más se abisma;
abre otro túnel más bajo tus flores
para hacer subterráneos mis amores.

36

[UNDERTAKER AND CEMETERY]

Final tailor of crystal and pinewood;
give me a suit the height of a rose,
so I fit in a prism, no, I would choke,
no, so I fit in a fine diamond.
Neighborhood patio that neighbors abandon,
where the final weight sinks deeper below;
your flowers open a tunnel lower down
to bury all my loves underground.

TED GENOWAYS

[GUERRA DE ESTÍO]

¡Oh combate imposible de la pita
con la que en torno mío luz avanza!
Su bayoneta, aunque incurriendo en lanza,
en vano con sus filos se concita;
como la de elipsoides ya crinita,
geométrica chumbera, nada alcanza:
lista la luz me toma sobre el huerto,
y a cañonazos de cigarras muerto.

[SUMMER WAR]

    Oh impossible combat of the agave
    around which my light advances!
    Your bayonet, although worthy of a lance,
    stirs in vain with your cutting blades;
    like that of ellipsoids now drawn into shade,
    the geometric prickly pear reaches
    for air: ready, the light takes me over the faded
    garden patch and cannon fire of cicadas.

TED GENOWAYS

EL RAYO QUE NO CESA
(1936)

THE UNENDING LIGHTNING
(1936)

1

[UN CARNÍVORO CUCHILLO]

Un carnívoro cuchillo
de ala dulce y homicida
sostiene un vuelo y un brillo
alrededor de mi vida.

Rayo de metal crispado
fulgentemente caído,
picotea mi costado
y hace en él un triste nido.

Mi sien, florido balcón
de mis edades tempranas,
negra está, y mi corazón,
y mi corazón con canas.

Tal es la mala virtud
del rayo que me rodea,
que voy a mi juventud
como la luna a la aldea.

Recojo con las pestañas
sal del alma y sal del ojo
y flores de telarañas
de mis tristezas recojo.

¿Adónde iré que no vaya
mi perdición a buscar?
Tu destino es de la playa
y mi vocación del mar.

Descansar de esta labor
de huracán, amor o infierno,
no es posible, y el dolor
me hará mi pesar eterno.

1

[A KNIFE THAT EATS FLESH]

A knife that eats flesh, and
sports a lovely homicidal wing,
keeps up its flying
and its light around my life.

Lightning bolt like shivering metal
that flashes down suddenly—
it digs into my side
and makes a red nest in there.

My temples, the flowery balcony
of my early ages,
are black; it is my heart—
my heart that's turning gray.

The evil strength of this lightning
all around me is so strong
that I go back to my youth
like the moon toward a village.

With my eyelashes I gather
salt from the soul and salt from the eye
and I gather cobweb
flowers from my grief.

Where can I go so that
I won't find my destruction?
You have a place on the sand,
and I am heading for the sea.

And to rest from this work
of tornadoes, love or hell,
is unthinkable, and the pain
will make the sorrow go on and on.

Pero al fin podré vencerte,
ave y rayo secular,
corazón, que de la muerte
nadie ha de hacerme dudar.

Sigue, pues, sigue, cuchillo,
volando, hiriendo. Algún día
se pondrá el tiempo amarillo
sobre mi fotografía.

But finally I will beat you,
bird, endless lightning,
heart, because no one
can shake my belief in death.

Go on then, knife, keep on
flying, giving wounds. One day
time will turn yellow
on top of my photograph.

ROBERT BLY

2

[*NO CESARÁ ESTE RAYO*]

¿No cesará este rayo que me habita
el corazón de exasperadas fieras
y de fraguas coléricas y herreras
donde el metal más fresco se marchita?

¿No cesará esta terca estalactita
de cultivar sus duras cabelleras
como espadas y rígidas hogueras
hacia mi corazón que muge y grita?

Este rayo ni cesa ni se agota:
de mí mismo tomó su procedencia
y ejercita en mí mismo sus furores.

Esta obstinada piedra de mí brota
y sobre mí dirige la insistencia
de sus lluviosos rayos destructores.

2

[WILL THIS BEAM OF LIGHT]

Will this beam of light go on forever
installing enraged animals inside me
and forges mad with anger and blacksmiths
where even the most delicate metal soon folds?

Will this tenacious stalactite never stop
nourishing its long hair stiff
as swords or
inside my heart that is bellows and cries out?

This beam of light will go on forever and never stop
because it pulls its power out of me
and sharpens off its madnesses in me.

This obstinate rock pushes its bud out of me
and it aims the insistent power of its lightnings,
deadly and rainy, straight at me.

TIMOTHY BALAND AND ROBERT BLY

3

Guiando un tribunal de tiburones,
como con dos guadañas eclipsadas,
con dos cejas tiznadas y cortadas
de tiznar y cortar los corazones,

en el mío has entrado, y en él pones
una red de raíces irritadas,
que avariciosamente acaparadas
tiene en su territorio sus pasiones.

Sal de mi corazón del que me has hecho
un girasol sumiso y amarillo
al dictamen solar que tu ojo envía:

un terrón para siempre insatisfecho,
un pez embotellado y un martillo
harto de golpear en la herrería.

[WHILE YOU WERE GUIDING HOME A SCHOOL OF SHARKS]

While you were guiding home a school of sharks
as if you held two eclipsed scythes in hand,
as if you held two eyebrows cut with sand
from cutting and from sanding hearts on land,

you entered in my cave, and in it place
a net of irritated slicing roots
that keep their passions as forbidden fruits
in total greed in this unentered space.

Now leave my heart from which you made for me
a yellow sunflower, a submissive plant,
your eye sent out by your sunhot command:

a plot of land always in misery,
a bottled fish, a hammer in a hand
weary of pounding iron until it can't.

WILLIS BARNSTONE

4

Me tiraste un limón, y tan amargo,
con una mano cálida, y tan pura,
que no menoscabó su arquitectura
y probé su amargura sin embargo.

Con el golpe amarillo, de un letargo
dulce pasó a una ansiosa calentura
mi sangre, que sintió la mordedura
de una punta de seno duro y largo.

Pero al mirarte y verte la sonrisa
que te produjo el limonado hecho,
a mi voraz malicia tan ajena,

se me durmió la sangre en la camisa,
y se volvió el poroso y áureo pecho
una picuda y deslumbrante pena.

4

You threw me a lemon, oh it was sour,
with a warm hand, that was so pure
it never damaged the lemon's architecture.
I tasted the sourness anyway.

With that yellow blow, my blood moved
from a gentle laziness into an anguished
fever, for my blood felt the bite
from a long and firm tip of a breast.

Yet glancing at you and seeing the smile
which that lemon-colored event drew from you,
so far from my dishonorable fierceness,

my blood went to sleep in my shirt,
and the soft and golden breast turned
to a baffling pain with a long beak.

ROBERT BLY

5

Tu corazón, una naranja helada
con un dentro sin luz de dulce miera
y una porosa vista de oro: un fuera
venturas prometiendo a la mirada.

Mi corazón, una febril granada
de agrupado rubor y abierta cera,
que sus tiernos collares te ofreciera
con una obstinación enamorada.

¡Ay, qué acontecimiento de quebranto
ir a tu corazón y hallar un hielo
de irreductible y pavorosa nieve!

Por los alrededores de mi llanto
un pañuelo sediento va de vuelo,
con la esperanza de que en él lo abreve.

5

[YOUR HEART?—IT IS A FROZEN ORANGE]

Your heart?—it is a frozen orange,
inside it has juniper oil but no light
and a porous look like gold: an outside
promising risks to the man who looks.

My heart is a fiery pomegranate,
its scarlets clustered, and its wax opened,
which could offer you its tender beads
with the stubbornness of a man in love.

Yes, what an experience of sorrow it is
to go to your heart and find a frost
made of primitive and terrifying snow!

A thirsty handkerchief flies through the air
along the shores of my weeping,
hoping that he can drink in my tears.

ROBERT BLY

[UMBRÍO POR LA PENA, CASI BRUNO]

Umbrío por la pena, casi bruno,
porque la pena tizna cuando estalla,
donde yo no me hallo no se halla
hombre más apenado que ninguno.

Sobre la pena duermo solo y uno,
pena es mi paz y pena mi batalla,
perro que ni me deja ni se calla,
siempre a su dueño fiel, pero importuno.

Cardos y penas me llevo por corona,
cardos y penas siembran sus leopardos
y no me dejan bueno hueso alguno.

No podrá con la pena mi persona
rodeada de penas y de cardos:
¡cuánto penar para morirse uno!

6

[OVERSHADOWED BY PAIN, NEARLY BLACK]

Overshadowed by pain, nearly black,
because pain soots when it explodes,
where I am not, there is not
the most tormented man alive.

I sleep single and alone on the pain,
pain is my peace and pain my battle:
a dog that neither deserts nor lies quiet,
always faithful but a pest to his master.

Thistles and pain I wear as a crown,
thistles and pain sow leopards
that do not leave an uncrushed bone for me.

Surrounded by pain and thistles
my body can bear no more.
So much suffering only to die!

TED GENOWAYS

7

[DESPUÉS DE HABER CAVADO ESTE BARBECHO]

Después de haber cavado este barbecho
me tomaré un descanso por la grama
y beberé del agua que en la rama
su esclava nieve aumenta en mi provecho.

Todo el cuerpo me huele a recienhecho
por el jugoso fuego que lo inflama
y la creación que adoro se derrama
a mi mucha fatiga como un lecho.

Se tomará un descanso el hortelano
y entretendrá sus penas combatido
por el salubre sol y el tiempo manso.

Y otra vez, inclinando cuerpo y mano,
seguirá ante la tierra perseguido
por la sombra del último descanso.

7

After having dug up this fallow site
I'll lie down on the ordinary grass
and drink some water which in branches pass
and grow from slave snow to my appetite.

And my whole body smells of someone born
today with juicy fire inflaming lead,
and the creation I adore is borne
flowing to my fatigue as to a bed.

This plain farmhand will also take his rest,
and though oppressed will entertain his grief
with healing sun and weather mildly tame.

Then up again, bending his hands and chest,
he'll journey on the earth with no relief
before the shadow of the final frame.

WILLIS BARNSTONE

8

[*POR TU PIE, LA BLANCURA MÁS BAILABLE*]

Por tu pie, la blancura más bailable,
donde cesa en diez partes tu hermosura,
una paloma sube a tu cintura,
baja a la tierra un nardo interminable.

Con tu pie vas poniendo lo admirable
del nácar en ridícula estrechura
y a donde va tu pie va la blancura,
perro sembrado de jazmín calzable.

A tu pie, tan espuma como playa,
arena y mar me arrimo y desarrimo
y al redil de su planta entrar procuro.

Entro y dejo que el alma se me vaya
por la voz amorosa del racimo:
pisa mi corazón que ya es maduro.

2

[FROM YOUR FEET WHERE LOVELINESS ENDS]

From your feet where loveliness ends
in ten parts of danceable whiteness,
a dove climbs up to your waist
flowing earthward in unending spikenard.

Your feet make the essence of nacre
seem so absurdly narrow that wherever
they go whiteness patters along—
a dog shedding anklets of jasmine.

I'm the surf and spume at your toes,
both sea wash and sand sift seeking
the way to your sheepcote soles.

There I'll enter, letting my soul slip
into the loving voice of grapes to say,
"Trample my heart, it's already ripe."

EDWIN HONIG

Fuera menos penado si no fuera
nardo tu tez para mi vista, nardo,
cardo tu piel para mi tacto, cardo,
tuera tu voz para mi oído, tuera.

Tuera es tu voz para mi oído, tuera,
y ardo en tu voz y en tu alrededor ardo,
y tardo a arder lo que a ofrecerte tardo
miera, mi voz para la tuya miera.

Zarza es tu mano si la tiento, zarza,
ola tu cuerpo si lo alcanzo, ola,
cerca una vez, pero un millar no cerca.

Garza es mi pena, esbelta y triste garza,
sola como un suspiro y un ay, sola,
terca en su error y en su desgracia terca.

9

It would be less painful
were your face not jasmine to my sight, jasmine,
thistle to my touch, thistle, your skin,
your voice crabapple to my ear, crabapple.

Your voice crabapple to my ear, crabapple,
and I burn in your voice, in your company burn,
and I hesitate to burn what I hesitate to offer,
my voice, juniper oil, for yours, juniper oil.

Your hand a thorn if I touch it, a thorn,
your body the tide if I reach for it, the tide,
once it draws near but is a thousand times gone.

My grief is a heron, a sad slender heron,
alone as a breath, and alone as a sigh,
headstrong in your error and in your woe headstrong.

TED GENOWAYS

[*TENGO ESTOS HUESOS HECHOS A LAS PENAS*]

Tengo estos huesos hechos a las penas
y a las cavilaciones estas sienes:
pena que vas, cavilación que vienes
como el mar de la playa a las arenas.

Como el mar de la playa a las arenas,
voy en este naufragio de vaivenes,
por una noche oscura de sartenes
redondas, pobres, tristes y morenas.

Nadie me salvará de este naufragio
si no es tu amor, la tabla que procuro,
si no es tu voz, el norte que pretendo.

Eludiendo por eso el mal presagio
de que ni en ti siquiera habré seguro,
voy entre pena y pena sonriendo.

[I HAVE ACCUSTOMED THESE BONES TO GRIEF]

I have accustomed these bones to grief
and these temples to deception:
grief goes, deception comes
like the sea from sand to beach.

Like the sea from beach to sand
I go from this wavering shipwreck
through a dark night, poor, black,
and sad as a round cast-iron pan.

If your love is not the plank I clench,
if your voice is not the north I follow,
no one will save me from this wreck.

So I go on eluding the dark omen
that I will never be safe in you,
smiling from heartache to heartache.

TED GENOWAYS

11

Te mueres de casta y de sencilla:
estoy convicto, amor, estoy confeso
de que, raptor intrépido de un beso,
yo te libé la flor de la mejilla.

Yo te libé la flor de la mejilla,
y desde aquella gloria, aquel suceso,
tu mejilla, de escrúpulo y de peso,
se te cae deshojada y amarilla.

El fantasma del beso delincuente
el pómulo te tiene perseguido,
cada vez más patente, negro y grande.

Y sin dormir estás, celosamente,
vigilando mi boca ¡con qué cuido!
para que no se vicie y se desmande.

11

It kills me, you're so pure and chaste:
though I confess, my love, I'm guilty,
I snatched that kiss; yes, it was I
who sipped the flower of your face.

I sipped the flower of your face,
and since that great day and deed
your face, so weighty and so scrupulous,
droops, falling like a yellow leaf.

The ghost of that delinquent kiss
now haunts your cheekbone, growing ever
darker, heavy and immense.

How jealously you stay awake!
How zealously you watch my lips
against (God forbid) another break!

EDWIN HONIG

[*UNA QUERENCIA TENGO POR TU ACENTO*]

Una querencia tengo por tu acento,
una apetencia por tu compañía
y una dolencia de melancolía
por la ausencia del aire de tu viento.

Paciencia necesita mi tormento,
urgencia de tu garza galanía,
tu clemencia solar mi helado día,
tu asistencia la herida en que lo cuento.

¡Ay querencia, dolencia y apetencia!:
tus sustanciales besos, mi sustento,
me faltan y me muero sobre mayo.

Quiero que vengas, flor desde tu ausencia,
a serenar la sien del pensamiento
que me desahoga en mí su eterno rayo.

12

I have an affection for your voice,
and a desire for your company
but a complaint of melancholy
for the absence of your presence.

My torment necessitates patience,
urgency of your blue-eyed beauty,
your mercy to pave my chilly day,
your aid in which I relate the malevolence.

Ay affection, complaint and desire!
your substantial kisses, my sustenance,
are lacking and I'm dying about May.

To calm my brow of suspicious thoughts, flower,
I want you to come from your absence
and save me from its endless calamity.

GEOFFREY HOLIDAY

[*MI CORAZÓN NO PUEDE CON LA CARGA*]

Mi corazón no puede con la carga
de su amorosa y lóbrega tormenta
y hasta mi lengua eleva la sangrienta
especie clamorosa que lo embarga.

Ya es corazón mi lengua lenta y larga,
mi corazón ya es lengua larga y lenta. . . .
¿Quieres contar sus penas? Anda y cuenta
los dulces granos de la arena amarga.

Mi corazón no puede más de triste:
con el flotante espectro de un ahogado
vuela en la sangre y se hunde sin apoyo.

Y ayer, dentro del tuyo, me escribiste
que de nostalgia tienes inclinado
medio cuerpo hacia mí, medio hacia el hoyo.

13

[MY HEART CAN'T GO ON ANY LONGER]

My heart can't go on any longer
putting up with its love-mad and murky storm,
and it raises to my tongue the blood-filled
noisy thing that weighs it down.

Now my tongue, slow and long, is a heart,
and my heart is a tongue, long and slow. . . .
You want to count up the pain? Go out and count
the sweet grains of the bitter sand.

My heart can't stand this sadness anymore:
it flies in my blood, along with the floating
ghost of a drowned man, and goes down all alone.

And yesterday, you wrote from your heart
that you have a touch of homesickness—
half for my body, half for the grave.

TIMOTHY BALAND

14

Silencio de metal triste y sonoro,
espadas congregando con amores
en el fina de huesos destructores
de la región volcánica del toro.

Una humedad de femenino oro
que olió puso en su sangre resplandores,
y refugió un bramido entre las flores
como un huracanado y vasto lloro.

De amorosas y cálidas cornadas
cubriendo está los trebolares tiernos
con el dolor de mil enamorados.

Bajo su piel las furias refugiadas
son en el nacimiento de sus cuernos
pensamientos de muerte edificados.

14

Sad, sonorous, silence of metal,
swords gathering with love
atop the destructive
bones of the volcanic snout of the bull.

He smelled an oasis of feminine
gold that put splendor in his blood,
and he sheltered a howl amid
flowers like a hurricaning and vast lament.

He is covering the tender clover
of loving and hot gorings
with the pain of a thousand lovers.

Under his skin, furies are harbored
and in the undergrowth of his horns
are thoughts forged by murder.

TED GENOWAYS

Me llamo barro aunque Miguel me llame.
Barro es mi profesión y mi destino
que mancha con su lengua cuanto lame.

Soy un triste instrumento del camino.
Soy una lengua dulcemente infame
a los pies que idolatro desplegada.

Como un nocturno buey de agua y barbecho
que quiere ser criatura idolatrada,
embisto a tus zapatos y a sus alrededores,
y hecho de alfombras y de besos hecho
tu talón que me injuria beso y siembro de flores.

Coloco relicarios de mi especie
a tu talón mordiente, a tu pisada,
y siempre a tu pisada me adelanto
para que tu impasible pie desprecie
todo el amor que hacia tu pie levanto.

Más mojado que el rostro de mi llanto,
cuando el vidrio lanar del hielo bala,
cuando el invierno tu ventana cierra
bajo a tus pies un gavilán de ala,
de ala manchada y corazón de tierra.
Bajo a tus pies un ramo derretido
de humilde miel pataleada y sola,
un despreciado corazón caído
en forma de alga y en figura de ola.

Barro en vano me invisto de amapola,
barro en vano vertiendo voy mis brazos,
barro en vano te muerdo los talones,
dándote a malheridos aletazos
sapos como convulsos corazones.

15

I call myself clay though Miguel is my name.
Clay is my profession and my destiny
whose tongue stains as long as it licks at time.

I am a sad instrument of the road's way.
I am but an infamous tongue sweetly warm
laid out at feet I idolize and adore.

Like a sad ox of floods and fallow places
that wants to be a venerated creature
I fawn upon your shoes and your surrounds
and, made for walking over and for kisses,
I kiss and strew with flowers the heel that wounds.

I place a token of my species
at your biting heel, at your tread,
and always at your step I flit
lest your impassive foot despise
all the love I raise toward it.

More than by weeping my face is wet,
when frozen glass wool bleats
and in winter when your window is shut
like a thistle's wing I fall at your feet,
a soiled wing of earth the heart.
At your feet I grovel a branch smitten
by love of lowly honey trampled and alone,
a heart despised and fallen
shaped like seaweed and an aspect of ocean.

Clay, I dress myself in vain
as poppy, in vain see my arms
empty, vainly your heels I bite,
giving them savage blows and storms,
angry words like a raging heart.

Apenas si me pisas, si me pones
la imagen de tu huella sobre encima,
se despedaza y rompe la armadura
de arrope bipartido que me ciñe la boca
en carne viva y pura,
pidiéndote a pedazos que la oprima
siempre tu pie de liebre libre y loca.

Su taciturna nata se arracima,
los sollozos agitan su arboleda
de lana cerebral bajo tu paso.
Y pasas, y se queda
incendiando su cera de invierno ante el ocaso,
mártir, alhaja y pasto de la rueda.

Harto de someterse a los puñales
circulantes del carro y la pezuña,
teme del barro un parto de animales
de corrosiva piel y vengativa uña.

Teme que el barro crezca en un momento,
teme que crezca y suba y cubra tierna,
tierna y celosamente
tu tobillo de junco, mi tormento,
teme que inunde el nardo de tu pierna
y crezca más y ascienda hasta tu frente.

Teme que se levante huracanado
del blando territorio del invierno
y estalle y truene y caiga diluviado
sobre tu sangre duramente tierno.

Teme un asalto de ofendida espuma
y teme un amoroso cataclismo.

Antes que la sequía lo consuma
el barro ha de volverte de lo mismo.

You make me suffer if you crush me, set
the imprint of your foot upon me,
it breaks my heart and destroys the mesh
of honeycomb that encircles my throat
in pure and living flesh,
loving you madly it ever oppresses me
your free and reckless clover foot.

Its silent perfection is united,
sobbing shakes its tree
of cerebral wool beneath your tread.
You pass, and it remains
burning its winter's wax before the sunset,
martyr, jewel and nourishment of seasons.

Tired of yielding to the whirling
knives of the wagon and the hoof,
from clay beware a spawn of avenging
beasts with corrosive skin and claws.

Beware for clay renews itself almost instantly,
beware lest it grow and rise and cover
softly, softly and jealously
your slender ankle, my torment of woe,
beware lest it drown the perfume of your
leg and growing more rise to your brow.

Beware lest it raise a hurricane
in the mild territory of winter
and explode and thunder and rain
upon your blood harshly tender.

Beware an assault of angry spume
and a gentle amorous profusion.

Before the drought consume
you clay must to clay return.

GEOFFREY HOLIDAY

[*SI LA SANGRE TAMBIÉN, COMO EL CABELLO*]

Si la sangre también, como el cabello,
con el dolor y el tiempo encaneciera,
mi sangre, roja hasta el carbunclo, fuera
pálida hasta el temor y hasta el destello.

Desde que me conozco me querello
tanto de tanto andar de fiera en fiera
sangre, y ya no es mi sangre una nevera
porque la nieve no se ocupa de ello.

Si el tiempo y el dolor fueran de plata
surcada como van diciendo quienes
a sus obligaciones y verdugas

Reliquias dan lugar, como la nata,
mi corazón tendría ya las sienes
espumosas de canas y de arrugas.

16

[IF BLOOD TOO, LIKE HAIR]

If blood too, like hair,
with sorrow and time grew white
my blood, now red as a garnet,
would grow pale as a sparkle, as fear.

Knowing me, I would complain
of so much zealous moving in my zealous
blood. My blood is no longer an ice-house
since in it ice has not yet frozen.

If time and pain, as if made of liquid silver,
were given the opportunity
to go around talking to their thankful

and executed relics, like lathered
cream, my heart would now have frothy
temples of gray hair and wrinkles.

TED GENOWAYS

[EL TORO SABE AL FIN DE LA CORRIDA]

El toro sabe al fin de la corrida,
donde prueba su chorro repentino,
que el sabor de la muerte es el de un vino
que el equilibrio impide de la vida.

Respira corazones por la herida
desde un gigante corazón vecino,
y su vasto poder de piedra y pino
cesa debilitado en la caída.

Y como el toro tú, mi sangre astada,
que el cotidiano cáliz de la muerte,
edificado con un turbio acero,

vierte sobre mi lengua un gusto a espada
diluida en un vino espeso y fuerte
desde mi corazón donde me muero.

[THE BULL KNOWS AT THE END OF THE FIGHT]

The bull knows at the end of the fight
in which it tastes its sudden gush
that a wine with the taste of death
impedes life and unbalances it.

Hearts breathe through the wound
from an immense neighboring one,
and its vast power of pine and stone
falls helplessly weak to the sand.

And like the bull you, my proud blood,
the bitter cup of daily dying
imbibed by the spirit turbidly,

spills on my tongue a taste of sword
diluted by a strong thick wine pulsing
from my heart where I shall die.

GEOFFREY HOLIDAY

[YA DE SU CREACIÓN, TAL VEZ, ALHAJA]

Ya de su creación, tal vez, alhaja
algún sereno aparte campesino
el agarrobo, el haya, el roble, el pino
que ha de dar la materia de mi caja.

Ya, tal vez, la combate y la trabaja
el talador con ímpetu asesino
y, tal vez, por la cuesta del camino
sangrando sube y resonando baja.

Ya, tal vez, la reduce a geometría,
a pliegos aplanados quien apresta
el último refugio a todo vivo.

Y cierta y sin tal vez, la tierra umbría
desde la eternidad está dispuesta
a recibir mi adiós definitivo.

[PERHAPS NOW, OF THEIR OWN VOLITION]

Perhaps now, of their own volition,
men adorn some serene country treeline
with the carob, the beech, the oak, the pine,
that will supply the timber for my coffin.

Now, perhaps, the lumberjack battles
and works it with murderous blows,
and, perhaps, along the slope of the road
it stands bleeding then resounding falls.

Now, perhaps, he reduces it to geometry,
to flat planks, he who readies
the last refuge of all those now alive.

And certainly, not perhaps, and for eternity
the dark earth is ready
to receive my definitive goodbye.

TED GENOWAYS

19

[*YO SÉ QUE VER Y OÍR A UN TRISTE ENFADA*]

Yo sé que ver y oír a un triste enfada,
cuando se viene y va de la alegría,
como un mar meridiano a una bahía,
a una región esquiva y desolada.

Lo que he sufrido y nada todo es nada
para lo que me queda todavía
que sufrir el rigor de esa agonía
de andar de este cuchillo a aquella espada.

Me callaré, me apartaré si puedo
con mi constante pena instante, plena,
a donde no has de oírme ni he de verte.

Me voy, me voy, me voy, pero me quedo,
pero me voy, desierto y sin arena:
adiós, amor, adiós hasta la muerte.

[I KNOW TO SEE AND HEAR A SAD VEXATION]

I know to see and hear a sad vexation
when one comes and goes from joy,
like a dazzling sea to a bay,
to a cold and desolate region.

What I have suffered is nothing compared
to what still is mine to suffer,
the harshness of this torture
of walking from this knife to that sword.

I will say no more but retreat if I can
with my constant pressing pain, complete,
to where you needn't hear me nor I you discern.

I'm going, I'm dying, but still I endure,
but I'm going without sand a desert;
adieu, love until death, adieu.

GEOFFREY HOLIDAY

20

[NO ME CONFORMO, NO: ME DESESPERO]

No me conformo, no: me desespero
como si fuera un huracán de lava
en el presidio de una almendra esclava
o en el penal colgante de un jilguero.

Besarte fue besar un avispero
que me clava al tormento y me desclava
y cava un hovo funebra y lo cava
dentro del corazón donde me muero.

No me conformo, no: ya es tanto y tanto
idolatrar la imagen de tu beso
y perseguir el curso de tu aroma.

Un enterrado vivo por el llanto,
una revolución dentro de un hueso,
un rayo soy sujeto a una redoma.

[NO. I WILL NOT CONFORM. BUT I DESPAIR]

No. I will not conform. But I despair
as if I were a hurricane of lava
locked in the fortress of an enslaved guava,
a hummingbird clawing to a hanging hair.

To kiss you was to kiss a hornet nest
that nails me to this torment and unnails
me; digging out a funeral pit, it sails
into my heart where in my death I rest.

No. I will not conform. I've tried so long
to worship the illusion of your kiss
and trail behind the curse of your rich smell.

And now my body buried live and wrong,
rebelling in its bones, I boil and hiss,
a lightning flash—but dead in glassy hell.

WILLIS BARNSTONE

[*¿RECUERDAS AQUEL CUELLO, HACES MEMORIA?*]

¿Recuerdas aquel cuello, haces memoria
del privilegio aquel, de aquel aquello
que era, almenadamente blanco y bello,
una almena de nata giratoria?

Recuerdo y no recuerdo aquella historia
de marfil expirado en un cabello,
donde aprendió a ceñir el cisne cuello
y a vocear la nieve transitoria.

Recuerdo y no recuerdo aquel cogollo
de extrangulable hielo femenino
como una lacteada y breve vía.

Y recuerdo aquel beso sin apoyo
que quedó entre mi boca y el camino
de aquel cuello, aquel beso y aquel día.

[DO YOU RECALL THAT NECK, A MEMORY AGO?]

Do you recall that neck, a memory ago
of privilege, and other times so full
it was almondly white and beautiful,
an almond of gyrating cream and flow?

I do recall and don't recall that glow
of ivory expiring in a hair
where the swan neck learned how to rope its glare
and scream about the transitory snow.

I do recall and don't recall that head
of strangulatable and female ice
like a congealing, brief, and milky way.

And I recall that unprotected kiss
that stuck inside my mouth, and then the road
into that neck, that kiss, that sudden day.

WILLIS BARNSTONE

22

Vierto la red, esparzo la semilla
entre ovas, aguas, surcos y amapolas,
sembrando a secas y pescando a solas
de corazón ansioso y de mejilla.

Espero a que recaiga en esta arcilla
la lluvia con sus crines y sus colas,
relámpagos sujetos a las olas
desesperando espero en esta orilla.

Pero transcurren lunas y más lunas,
aumenta de mirada mi deseo
y no crezco en espigas o en pescados.

Lunas de perdición como ningunas,
porque sólo recojo y sólo veo
piedras como diamantes eclipsados.

22

[I CAST THE NET, SCATTER THE SEED'S STOCK]

I cast the net, scatter the seed's stock
between algae, water, furrows, and poppies red,
sowing merely and fishing in solitude
with an anxious heart and cheek.

I await, in this clay, what falls back;
the bucking rain with its manes and tails,
lightning imprisoned by the waves' swell
and, despairing, wait at the river's bank.

But more moons pass and time passes
increasing with a glance my desire
and I grow neither by corn nor fishes.

Moons of violent unrestrained love, moons
like nothing, because I only see and gather,
like eclipsed diamonds, worthless stones.

GEOFFREY HOLIDAY

[COMO EL TORO HE NACIDO PARA EL LUTO]

Como el toro he nacido para el luto
y el dolor, como el toro estoy marcado
por un hierro infemal en el costado
y por varón en la ingle con un fruto.

Como el toro lo encuentra diminuto
todo mi corazón desmesurado,
y del rostro del beso enamorado,
como el toro a tu amor se lo disputo.

Como el toro me crezco en el castigo,
la lengua en corazón tengo bañada
y llevo al cuello un vendaval sonoro.

Como el toro te sigo y te persigo,
y dejas mi deseo en una espada,
como el toro burlado, como el toro.

[LIKE THE BULL I WAS BORN FOR DOOM AND PAIN]

Like the bull I was born for doom and pain,
like the bull I parade the burning mark,
the infernal wound under my ribs. The stark
fruit of a man stabs in my groin insane.

Like the bull no arena can contain
my heart that finds all others small. The flow
of loving kisses floors me in its tow.
Like the bull I argue for your love in vain.

Like the bull I thrive on punishment,
My tongue is washed in my own heart.
I hoard a thundering seawind in my leather skull.

Like the bull I seek you and cannot relent,
but my desire you welded to a sword,
like the bull become a fool, like the bull.

WILLIS BARNSTONE

24

[FATIGA TANTO ANDAR SOBRE LA ARENA]

Fatiga tanto andar sobre la arena
descorazonadora de un desierto,
tanto vivir en la ciudad de un puerto
si el corazón de barcos no se llena.

Angustia tanto el son de la sirena
oído siempre en un anclado huerto,
tanto la campanada por el muerto
que en el otoño y en la sangre suena,

que un dulce tiburón, que una manada
de inofensivos cuernos recentales,
habitándome días, meses y años,

ilustran mi garganta y mi mirada
de sollozos de todos los metales
y de fieras de todos los tamaños.

24

It tires me so much to step
on sand disheartened by the desert;
so much to live in a town with a port
if the heart is empty of ships.

It worries me so much, the sound
of sirens, heard in an anchored orchard,
so much the bells tolling for the dead
in autumn, tolling in the blood,

that a sweet shark, that a herd
of harmless suckling sheep,
inhabiting my days, months and years,

light up my throat and my stare
with sobs of iron and steel,
and with all shape of wild creatures.

TED GENOWAYS

Al derramar tu voz su mansedumbre
de miel bocal, y al puro bamboleo,
en mis terrestres manos el deseo
sus rosas pone al fuego de costumbre.

Exasperado llego hasta la cumbre
de tu pecho de isla, y lo rodeo
de un ambicioso mar y un pataleo
de exasperados pétalos de lumbre.

Pero tú defiendes con murallas
de mis alteraciones codiciosas
de sumergirte en tierras y oceános.

Por piedra pura, indiferente, callas:
callar de piedra, que otras y otras rosas
me pones y me pones en las manos.

[TO THE POURING OF YOUR VOICE'S]

To the pouring of your voice's
honey-mouthed gentleness and pure
swaying at the ceremonial fire, desire
piles my dirt-crusted hands with roses.

Breathless, I reach the peak
of your island breast and surround it
with an ambitious sea and a footbeat
of breathless petals like sparks.

But you defend yourself from
my lustful moods with walls
that submerge you in oceans and lands.

Because you are pure stone,
indifferent, silent as stone, you pile
again and again roses in my hands.

TED GENOWAYS

[*POR UNA SENDA VAN LOS HORTELANOS*]

Por una senda van los hortelanos,
que es la sagrada hora del regreso,
con la sangre injuriada por el peso
de inviernos, primaveras y veranos.

Vienen de los esfuerzos sobrehumanos
y van a la canción, y van al beso,
y van dejando por el aire impreso
un olor de herramientas y de manos.

Por otra senda yo, por otra senda
que no conduce al beso aunque es la hora,
sino que merodea sin destino.

Bajo su frente tragica y tremenda,
un toro solo en la ribera llora
olvidando que es toro y masculino.

26

[THE PEASANTS RAMBLE DOWN A SINGLE PATH]

The peasants ramble down a single path
and at the holy hour of the return
their blood's insulted by the cold and burn
of winters, springs, and summers' wrath.

They come from superhuman aches and toil,
meander to a song and to a kiss,
and go on signing air with genesis
of hands, of iron tools, and reeking oil.

I walk another path, another now
not leading to a kiss, although it's time,
but to an unfixed, vagrant origin.

Under its tragic and tremendous brow
a bull alone weeps on a bed of slime,
forgetting it is bull and masculine.

WILLIS BARNSTONE

27

[LLUVIOSOS OJOS QUE LLUVIOSAMENTE]

Lluviosos ojos que lluviosamente
me hacéis penar: lluviosas soledades,
balcones de la rudas tempestades
que hay en mi corazón adolescente.

Corazón cada día más frecuente
en para idolatrar criar ciudades
de amor que caen de todas mis edades
babilónicamente y fatalmente.

Mi corazón, mis ojos sin consuelo,
metrópolis de atmósfera sombría
gastados por un río lacrimoso.

Ojos de ver y no gozar el cielo,
corazón de naranja cada día,
si más envejecido, más sabroso.

[RAINY EYES, LIKE STORM SHOWERS]

Rainy eyes, like storm showers,
you grieve me: rainy loneliness,
windows opened on rough tempests
in my adolescent heart.

Heart that each day must haunt
sprawling, love-filled cities
that fall prey to idolatry
fatally as biblical Babylon.

My heart, my inconsolable eyes:
one, a smoke-choked metropolis,
the other, spent by a tear-filled river.

Eyes see but cannot enjoy the sky;
heart like an orange, each sunrise,
though older, grows fuller of flavor.

TED GENOWAYS

[LA MUERTE, TODA LLENA DE AGUJEROS]

La muerte, toda llena de agujeros
y cuernos de su mislIlo desenlace,
bajo una piel de toro pisa y pace
un luminoso prado de toreros.

Volcánicos bramidos, humos fieros
de general amor por cuanto nace,
a llamaradas echa mientras hace
morir a los tranquilos ganaderos.

Ya puedes, amorosa fiera hambrienta,
pastar mi corazón, trágica grama,
si te gusta lo amargo de su asunto.

Un amor hacia todo me atormenta
como a ti, y hacia todo se derrama
mi corazón vestido de difunto.

28

[DEATH, ENCLOSED IN A BULL'S HIDE]

Death, enclosed in a bull's hide,
entirely full of holes and horn-
thrusts she made herself, stamps
and feeds on the bullfighters' luminous practice ground.

Fantastic roars, killing smoke
and flames shoot out with ecstatic love
for whatever is born, while all the time
death makes the tranquil ranchers die.

Go on, you love-mad animal, starved,
graze on my heart, that tragic grass,
if the bitterness of it all gives you pleasure.

Like you, I can't sleep, because I love
too many things, and my heart, dressed
like the dead, overflows toward the universe.

TIMOTHY BALAND

ELEGÍA

(En Orihuela, su pueblo y el mio, se me ha muerto como el rayo Ramon Sije, con quien tanto quería.)

Yo quiero ser, llorando el hortelano
de la tierra que ocupas y estercolas,
compañero del alma, tan temprano.

Alimentando lluvias, caracolas
y órganos mi dolor sin instrumento,
a las desalentadas amapolas

daré tu corazón por alimento.
Tanto dolor se agrupa en mi costado,
que por doler me duele hasta el aliento.

Un manotazo duro, un golpe helado,
un hachazo invisible y homicida,
un empujón brutal te ha derribado.

No hay extensión más grande que mi herida,
lloro me desventura y sus conjuntos
y siento más tu muerte que mi vida.

Ando sobre rastrojos de difuntos,
y sin calor de nadie y sin consuelo
voy de mi corazón a mis asuntos.

Temprano levantó la muerte el vuelo,
temprano madrugó la madrugada,
temprano estás rodando por el suelo.

No perdono a la muerte enamorada,
no perdono a la vida desatenta,
no perdono a la tierra ni a la nada.

29

ELEGY

Like lightning death struck my close friend Ramón Sijé in our home town of Orihuela.

Ramón, right now I want to be
the mournful friend who tends the ground
you fertilize and lie in, gave too soon.

Since this useless grief of mine
likes the taste of rain, snail shells, the organs of the body,
I'll go ahead and feed your heart

to the disheartened poppies.
Grief bunches up between my ribs,
each breath I take is painful.

The hard slap of a hand, an icy fist,
that violent, that fatal, unseen
blow of an ax has cut you down.

There's nothing big enough to stick my hurt in.
I cry anguished tears,
I feel your death more than my life.

I walk across the stubble of the dead:
no warmth, no consolation from a single body.
I leave this heart of mine behind and try to go on living.

Death flew away with you too early,
that morning came before it should have,
before your time you are in the ground.

Lovesick death will get no forgiveness out of me,
none for this thankless life,
none for the earth, nor for the black nothing.

En mis manos levanto una tormenta
de piedras, rayos y hachas estridentes
sedienta de catástrofes y hambrienta.

Quiero escarbar la tierra con los dientes,
quiero apartar la tierra parte a parte
a dentelladas secas y calientes.

Quiero minar la tierra hasta encontrarte
y besarte la noble calavera
y desamordazarte y regresarte.

Volverás a mi huerto y a mi higuera:
por los altos andamios de las flores
pajareará tu alma colmenera

de angelicales ceras y labores.
Volverás al arrullo de las rejas
de los enamorados labradores.

Alegrarás la sombra de mis cejas,
y tu sangre se irán a cada lado
disputando tu novia y las abejas.

Tu corazón, ya terciopelo ajado,
llama a un campo de almendras espumosas
mi avariciosa voz de enamorado.

A las aladas almas de las roasas
del almendro de nata te requiero,
que tenemos que hablar de muchas cosas,
compañero del alma, compañero.

10 de enero de 1936

In these hands of mine a storm made of rocks
is brewing, lightning, vicious axes
dry and starving for catastrophes.

I want to dig up the earth with my teeth,
I want to take dry, fiery bites
pulling it apart bit by bit.

I want to tear up the earth until I find you,
so I can kiss your noble skull,
unbandage your mouth, and bring you back to life.

You will come back to the fig tree in my backyard:
your soul will be at peace there,
high up among the blossoms, gathering

the wax and honey of angelic hives.
You'll come back to words whispered through
grillwork windows by romantic field hands.

You'll blow away the shadows on my brow,
and your woman and the bees will take
turns claiming your blood as theirs.

Your heart, now only crumpled velvet,
calls from a field of surf-like almond trees
to my voice, wanting and full of love.

And I call you to come to the milky
almond blossoms who are souls flying.
I miss you, Ramón. Ramón, we still have
so many things to talk about.

January 10, 1936

TIMOTHY BALAND

SONETO FINAL

Por desplumar arcángeles glaciales,
la nevada lilial de esbeltos dientes
es condenada al llanto de las fuentes
y al desconsuelo de los manantiales.

Por difundir su alma en los metales,
por dar el fuego al hierro sus orientes,
al dolor de los yunques inclementes
lo arrastran los herreros torrenciales.

Al doloroso trato de la espina,
al fatal desaliento de la rosa
y a la acción corrosiva de la muerte

arrojado me veo, y tanta ruina
no es por otra desgracia ni otra cosa
que por quererte y solo por quererte.

FINAL SONNET

For pulling the feathers from icy archangels
the lily-like snowstorm of slender teeth
is condemned to the weeping of the fountains
and the desolation of the running springs.

For diffusing its soul into metals,
for abandoning the sunrises to the iron,
the stormy blacksmiths drag away the fire
to the anguish of the brutal anvils.

I see myself rushing recklessly toward the painful
retribution of the thorn, to the fatal
discouragement of the rose, and the acidulous

power of death, and so much ruin
is not for any sin or any other thing
except loving you, only for loving you.

ROBERT BLY

THE WAR POEMS: 1936–1939

The Outbreak of War

The publication of "My Blood Is a Road" in the first issue of Pablo
Neruda's *Caballo verde* was a watershed for Miguel Hernández. It sig-
naled his final break from Ramón Sijé and the Orihuelan writers' group
and announced his interest in surrealist poetry. His alliance with Neruda
was made most explicit in the review he wrote of Neruda's *Residencia en
la tierra (Residence on Earth)* for the January 2, 1936, issue of *El sol*. Early
in the article, he revealed the profound effect that Neruda was having
on him:

> I need to communicate the enthusiasm that has trans-
> formed me since I have read *Residence on Earth*. I want to
> throw handfuls of sand in my eyes, to catch my fingers in
> doors, to climb to the peak of the most difficult and high
> pine. It would be the best way to express the stormy admira-
> tion that a poet of such giant size awakes in me. It is a danger
> for me to write about this book and it seems to me that I can
> say almost nothing of the enormity that I feel. Fearfully, I
> write.[1]

But soon, Hernández's temerity faded and his enthusiasm for Neruda's
poetics led him to challenge other poets to aspire to the heights of such
poetic invention:

> I am tired of so much pure and minor art. I long for the dis-
> ordered and chaotic confusion of the Bible, where I see
> grand spectacles, cataclysms, misfortunes, worlds upturned,
> and I hear screams and landslides of blood. I don't care for
> the puny voice that goes in ecstasy standing before a poplar,
> that fires off four little verses and believes that now every-
> thing has been done in poetry.
>
> Enough of the prudishness and syrupy-sweetness of
> poets acting like candymakers, all prim, all with sugared

---

1. Hernández, *Obra completa*, 3: 2152.

fingertips. I call on poets of Pablo Neruda's dimensions to
end such rhymed confectionery.[2]

Those "screams and landslides of blood" were apparent in "My Blood Is
a Road" and "Bloody Fate," in which the poet boldly proclaims, "I come,
blood on blood." The poems Hernández was writing during this period,
when coupled with his artistic declarations, were his public announce-
ment of his willingness to write on "impure" subjects, to write against
Catholic doctrine, and by so doing to imply political opposition to the
growing Fascist movement within Spain.

It will never be known for certain whether this sudden political
profile had anything to do with Hernández's apprehension in early Janu-
ary 1936, but what is certain is that as soon as he identified himself to a
group of Guardia Civil, he was met with violence.

The best record of this event appeared in *El socialista*, a socialist news-
paper in Madrid:

> On Monday, the 7th day of this month of January, the poet
> Miguel Hernández was passing the day on the outskirts
> of Jarama [outside Madrid], when he was detained by the
> Guardia Civil, and questioned; when asked what he was
> doing in that place, Miguel Hernández answered, smiling,
> that he was a writer and that he was there for pleasure. The
> humble clothes of our modest friend led the Guardia Civil to
> respond with violence, leading him to the barracks of San
> Fernando. During the journey, to hide the shame that pro-
> voked his detention, Miguel Hernández was furiously beaten
> with the butt of their rifles. Then they threatened him with
> death, saying: "If not for that woman walking behind us, we
> would beat you to a pulp."
>
> They entered the barracks and, without further explana-
> tion, the commander slapped his face. They followed with
> punches and took his keys from him after a thorough search,
> in which they encountered further, like terrible proof, a
> quarter-sheet of paper written with the name *Juan de oro*.
> The Guardia Civil of that place could not understand that a
> man with such a country air had written the title of a play.
> "This is an accomplice. Go ahead. Confess." He was held like

2. Ibid.: 2157.

this in the barracks, enduring beatings, insults, harassment, until he was allowed to telephone a friend in Madrid, who responded in person.[3]

From a letter written in the following weeks, we know the person Hernández contacted was Neruda, whose sway as Chilean consul secured his immediate release, but no explanation for the detention was ever given.[4] Less than ten days later, *El socialista* published the above description of his ordeal, together with a protest of such treatment, concluding:

> We are denouncing [such brutality] in this case, because Miguel Hernández is one of our most valiant young poets. But, how many atrocities as stupid and cruel as this are committed daily throughout Spain without anyone's knowledge![5]

The first name signed to this protest was Federico García Lorca. Others included Neruda, José Bergamín, Rafael Alberti, Manuel Altolaguirre, and Luis Cernuda. Lorca's strong sympathies with the socialist movement and his position in the list of protesters implied that he had much to do with the open letter, and may indeed have been the author.

This event had two unexpected effects on Hernández; first, it forced his already stirring political beliefs to the extreme left, but second, it brought him to the forefront of young poets in Spain. Here was a written endorsement, signed by all the prominent poets of the Generation of '27, proclaiming him "one of our most valiant young poets." But typical of his conflicted feelings, Hernández—only weeks after his beating at the hands of the Guardia Civil—wrote to Josefina's father, asking the opportunity to renew his relationship with her.

When Manuel Manresa replied allowing Hernández to write to his daughter, their love affair resumed with all the passion it had enjoyed before their estrangement nearly a year before. Soon, he revealed his growing hatred for the Fascist government as a result of his beating, writing, "Understand that since that day I feel hatred toward all the Guardia

3. Hernández, *Poesía y prosa de guerra*, 37–38.
4. "In the end, they allowed me to telephone to Madrid to my friend, the Chilean consul, and without giving me an explanation or an apology they set me free." Hernández, *Obra completa*, 3: 2374.
5. Hernández, *Poesía y prosa de guerra*, 38.

Civil, except your father, Josefina."[6] He made plans to return to Orihuela to visit her in late July.

On July 18, 1936—the date immortalized by one of Hernández's later sonnets—the Spanish civil war officially began. When he arrived in Orihuela, Hernández found his friends politically opposed to him and his work—such as the poem "Viento del Pueblo" ("Wind of the People," an early version of "Sentado sobre los muertos" ["Sitting upon the Dead"]). Still, he felt confident that the events of the war would not interfere in his resurgent love affair with Josefina. In the coming weeks, that illusion would be shattered, and the toll this bloody war would take on his friends from both his early life in Orihuela and his new life in Madrid soon became apparent.

On August 13, Manuel Manresa was killed by Republican sympathizers near Elda, a town where he was stationed with the Guardia Civil. Hernández volunteered to care for the family—Manresa's widow, Josefina, a teenage son, and three young daughters—and began investigating who was responsible and what support the family could expect from the state. On September 1, amid this turmoil, the Madrid newspaper *La voz* carried the following item:

> *Has García Lorca been assassinated?*
> Guadix. Rumours from the Córdoba front, which up to now have not been disproved, reveal the possible shooting of the great poet Federico García Lorca, on the orders of Colonel Cascajo.[7]

A week later, several Madrid newspapers carried the testimony of a Republican who had escaped from Granada to the front at Guadix. The man expressed his certainty that Lorca along with several other Republican sympathizers had been shot on August 19. The front page of *La voz* shouted: "THE EXECUTION OF THE GREAT POET GARCÍA LORCA HAS BEEN CONFIRMED."[8]

Most of Hernández's time that month was spent trying to make arrangements for the family of Manuel Manresa, but in a brief letter to a friend in Madrid, he asked mournfully, "Is it certain, is it certain about

6. Hernández, *Obra completa*, 3: 2374.
7. Gibson, 183.
8. Ibid., 184.

Federico García Lorca?"[9] Sometime that fall, Hernández would write his "Elegy" for Lorca, which reads in part:

> Of all the dead in elegies,
> not forgetting the echo of any,
> my tear-stained hand chooses one
> that has resonated most in my soul.
>
> Until yesterday he was called
> Federico García: now he is called dust.
> Yesterday he had a place under the sun
> but today he is put in a hole under the grass.[10]

More than ever before Hernández felt committed to the anti-Fascist cause. In September, he joined the Republican army.

The Soldier Poet

After a few months digging trenches around Madrid, Hernández was transferred to a propaganda unit within the Republican army and given the title "commissar of culture." The position was the direct result of a pair of poems published in *El mono azul (The Blue Overall)*, a publication of the Alliance of Anti-Fascist Intellectuals, whose name referred to the workclothes worn by many of the *campesino* Loyalists. The poems, later retitled "Sitting upon the Dead" and "Wind of the People," were part of a collection Hernández was planning, also entitled *Viento del Pueblo (Wind of the People)*.

At the end of November, the poems were printed in the government-published and distributed *Romancero de la guerra civil (Romances of the Civil War)*. The anthology was also sent abroad to try to capitalize on growing sympathies among European and American writers; it was the first time his work was introduced to an international community. Within Spain, Hernández traveled constantly, giving recitations to throngs of men at both fronts and on the Loyalist radio station. In January 1937, his poems and short prose pieces became regular features in *Al*

9. Hernández, *Obra completa*, 3: 2455.
10. Ibid., 1: 552.

ataque, the military newspaper distributed to all servicemen. Friend and critic T. Navarro Tomás wrote:

> [Hernández's] poems of war, written in camp, in the trenches, before the enemy, have appeared in the military magazine *Al ataque,* and have been reproduced in numerous public magazines. In many cases, his recitations exalting the spirits of his comrades have caused the camps to vibrate with ardent applause.[11]

On January 22, the poem "Sitting upon the Dead" (still under the title "Wind of the People") appeared in *El sol,* the largest daily newspaper of Madrid. It signaled the change that Hernández was poised to undergo: his transformation from the "shepherd poet" to the "soldier poet." Amid his frequent readings, he still managed to write over fifty poems and short prose pieces that appeared in every military publication possible—*Al ataque, Ayuda, La voz del combatiente, Frente sur,* even *A l'assaut,* the publication of the International Brigade. Hernández was now the unmistakable voice of the anti-Fascist cause.

On March 9, 1937, after months of trying to schedule a date, Hernández and Josefina Manresa were married and enjoyed a one-day honeymoon in Alicante. He made arrangements so they could live together in Jaén, but in less than six weeks Josefina's mother died and she was forced to return home to care for her siblings. Hernández wrote to her often, aching to see her, then soon received word from her that she was pregnant. The overpowering joy fueled the poem "Canción del esposo soldado" ("Song of the Soldier Husband"), which proclaims, "Our child will be born with a clenched fist," the salute of the Republican army.

In June, Hernández helped organize and participated in the Second International Congress of Anti-Fascist Writers, a conference of poets and writers sympathetic to the Loyalist cause. The event was a virtual who's who of 1930s literature: W. H. Auden, Malcolm Cowley, André Malraux, Pablo Neruda, Stephen Spender, César Vallejo, and the young Octavio Paz. Though he was respected among the visiting writers as the voice of the Spanish people, what Neruda called "a fighting word," Hernández's beloved Spain was losing out to Franco's Fascist army.[12] When Neruda told Miguel that he wanted to return to his apartment in Madrid to

11. Ibid., 548.
12. Neruda, 125, translated by St. Martin.

gather some of his books and personal belongings, Hernández borrowed a military van and drove his old mentor to the spacious "House of Flowers" building, near the entrance to the campus of the university. When they arrived, Neruda was shocked by what he found:

> Flak had knocked in the windows and chunks of the walls. The books had toppled off the shelves. It was impossible to find one's way in the rubble. I searched for things haphazardly. Oddly enough, the most useless, superfluous things had vanished, carried off by invading or defending forces. The pots and pans, the sewing machines, the dishes were there: they were scattered all over, but they had survived, yet there was not a trace of my consul's tail coat, my Polynesian masks, my Oriental knives.
>
> "War is as whimsical as dreams, Miguel."
>
> Miguel found some manuscripts of mine somewhere among the strewn papers. That chaos was a final door on my life. I said to Miguel, "I don't want to take anything with me."
>
> "Nothing? Not even one book?"
>
> "Not even one book."
>
> And we went back with the van empty.[13]

Though the Loyalist cause was clearly in decline, Hernández's reputation climbed sharply after the anti-Fascist conference. Early the next month, the government publisher Ediciones Españolas published *Poetas en la España leal (Poets in Loyalist Spain)* to commemorate the occasion. The slim volume of forty-four poems would bring international acclaim to the Spanish poets, and Hernández's two poems would bring him unexpected champions in William Carlos Williams and, in particular, the English poet Stephen Spender.

In late August, Hernández left with a small government-sponsored delegation to see the Fifth Festival of Soviet Theater. After nearly two months of attending banquets and other social events in Russia, he was sent almost directly to Teruel, where he was stationed on the front lines, seeing little action, but enduring the extreme cold of the long siege. Nearly exhausted from writing, fighting on the front, and the constant schedule of travel, Hernández began to suffer from debilitating headaches caused by "cerebral anemia." Even with Josefina expecting, he

13. Ibid., 133.

was too weak to write and did not learn of the birth of his son until he was shipped home for several weeks of rest cure.

Once there, Hernández recuperated and at last was able to hold his young son, Manuel Ramón Hernández Manresa (named for Josefina's father and Ramón Sijé). It would be the only extended time they would share. In October 1938, after months away from his family—on a constant tour of recitations with only occasional leaves—Hernández received word that his son, not yet a year old, had died of an intestinal disorder caused by malnutrition. The poems Hernández wrote during all of 1938 reveal his growing sense of despair. The increasing inevitability of a Fascist victory, the death of his son, and word that his deeply withdrawn wife had become pregnant again during one of his leaves left Hernández devastated. The poems of *El hombre acecha (Man Is a Hunter)* now complete, Hernández began keeping poems in a small notebook in October 1938, works that would eventually comprise *Cancionero y romancero de ausencias (The Songbook and Balladbook of Absences)*.

Ironically, at the depths of this depression, Hernández was becoming an international poet. The anthology published only months before, *Poets in Loyalist Spain,* had been hurriedly translated and published in the United States as . . . *and Spain Sings,* edited by M. J. Benardete and Rolfe Humphries. This little-known volume was the first translation of Hernández's work into English and, as fate would have it, the editors had selected William Carlos Williams to translate "Sitting upon the Dead" (as "Wind of the Village"). Though largely a rushed job, meant to turn public opinion in the waning days of the war, Williams's translation captures the hopeful spirit of Hernández's poem:

> If I was born of this earth,
> if I have issued from a womb
> wretched and impoverished,
> it was only that I might be
> the nightingale of misfortunes,
> echo of evil luck,
> to sing over and over
> for those who must hear . . . [14]

But by the time that song reached the world, Hernández was preparing to publish the collection *Man Is a Hunter,* with its poems of the lost

14. Benardete and Humphries, eds., . . . *and Spain Sings,* 14.

war and its images of trains and hospitals full of wartorn bodies, where blood rains from the skies and rises in huge deluges, "where even death could hardly bathe." The irony is especially stark in Stephen Spender's introduction to another anthology entitled *Poems for Spain* (which Spender coedited with John Lehmann), published in early 1939. Speaking of the Spanish poets in general, and quoting specifically from his own translation of Hernández's "Recoged esta voz," Spender said:

> [T]hey are defending a life and culture which they see threatened. Unless they both fight and write, they seem to say, there will be a future in which they are spiritually dead. Again, Hernandez [*sic*]:
> "A future of dust advances,
> a fate advances
> in which nothing will remain;
> nor stone on stone nor bone on bone."
> They have chosen death rather than that "future of dust."[15]

This statement now seems an eerie premonition. On March 29, two months after the birth of Hernández's second son and just weeks before *Man Is a Hunter* was scheduled for release, the Spanish civil war came to a close. Hernández went to the Chilean embassy to seek refuge, but Neruda had long since fled the country and the new consul was uncertain whether the Chilean government would still be able to grant Hernández and his family asylum. He returned home, where he spent three weeks with his family awaiting the fallout from the war. Seeing that his situation was worsening with the new Francist government, Hernández left a copy of *Man Is a Hunter* with Josefina and fled to seek asylum in Portugal.

He was able to cross the border covertly, but, short of money, he sold his blue suit to a man who handed him over to the Portuguese police, who turned him back to the border despite his pleas for political asylum. At Rosal de la Frontera, he was arrested by the Guardia Civil and beaten until "he pissed blood."[16] He was then taken back to Madrid under guard and held in Torrijos Prison.

15. Spender and Lehmann, eds., *Poems for Spain*, 8.
16. Barnstone, 272.

[POEMAS SUELTOS]
(1936)

[UNCOLLECTED POEMS]
(1936)

ELEGÍA

(En Orihuela, su pueblo y el mío, se ha quedado novia por casar la panadera de pan más trabajado y fino, que le han muerto la pareja del ya imposible esposo.)

Tengo ya el alma ronca y tengo ronco
el gemido de música traidora . . .
Arrímate a llorar conmigo a un tronco:

retírate conmigo al campo y llora
a la sangrienta sombra de un granado
desgarrado de amor como tú ahora.

Caen desde un cielo gris desconsolado,
caen ángeles cernidos para el trigo
sobre el invierno gris desocupado.

Arrímate, retírate conmigo:
vamos a celebrar nuestros dolores
junto al árbol del campo que te digo.

Panadera de espigas y de flores,
panadera lilial de piel de era,
panadera de panes y de amores.

No tienes ya en el mundo quien te quiera,
y ya tus desventuras y las mías
no tienen compañero, compañera.

Tórtola compañera de sus días,
que le dabas tus dedos cereales
y en su voz tu silencio entretenías.

Buscando abejas va por los panales
el silencio que ha muerto de repente
en su lengua de abejas torrenciales.

No esperes ver tu párpado caliente
ni tu cara dulcísima y morena
bajo los dos solsticios de su frente.

ELEGY

(In Orihuela, your town and mine, a fiancée has remained to marry the finest and hardest-working bread baker; that he has died couples her now with an impossible husband.)

I have already a hoarse soul and a hoarse
moan of traitorous music . . .
Lean close to cry with me against a trunk:

retreat with me to the field and cry
in the bloody shade of a pomegranate tree
torn by love like you are now.

They fall from an inconsolable gray sky,
angels fall, sievings of wheat
on the gray, vacant winter.

Lean close, retreat with me:
we are going to celebrate our pains
next to the tree in the field that I describe.

Baker of corn ears and flowers,
lily-white baker with skin like a threshing floor,
baker of bread and love.

Already in this world you're without the man who loves you,
and already my misfortune and yours,
my companion, have no companion.

Turtledove, companion of your days,
that you gave grain from your fingers
and in its voice you entertained your silence.

Looking for bees, your silence goes
by the honeycomb that has died suddenly
in its language of torrential bees.

You do not hope to see your hot eyelid
nor your sweetest and brown face
under the twin solstices of its brow.

El moribundo rostro de tu pena
se hiela y desendulza grado a grado
sin su labor de sol y de colmena.

Como una buena fiebre iba a tu lado,
como un rayo dispuesto a ser herida,
como un lirio de olor precipitado.

Y sólo queda ya de tanta vida
un cadáver de cera desmayada
y un silencio de abeja detenida.

¿Dónde tienes en esto la mirada
si no es descarriada por el suelo,
si no es por la mejilla trastornada?

Novia sin novio, novia sin consuelo,
te advierto entre barrancos y huracanes
tan extensa y tan sola como el cielo.

Corazón de relámpagos y afanes,
paginaba los libros de tus rosas,
apacentaba el hato de tus panes.

Ibas a ser la flor de las esposas,
y a pasos de relámpago tu esposo
se te va de las manos harinosas.

Echale, harina, un toro clamoroso
negro hasta cierto punto a tu menudo
vellón de lana blanco y silencioso.

A echar copos de harina yo te ayudo
y a sufrir por lo bajo, compañera,
viuda de cuerpo y de alma yo viudo.

La inplacable muerte nos espera
como un agua incesante y mal parida
a la vuelta de cada vidriera.

The dying face of your pain
freezes and unsweetens bit by bit
without its work of sun and beehive.

Like a good fever gone to your side,
like a ray ready to be wounded,
like an iris's reckless scent.

And already it is left with only as much life
as a dismayed, waxen corpse
and the silence of an imprisoned bee.

Where do you have in this the glance
if it is not misled by the ground,
if it is not upturned by the cheek?

Fiancée without fiancée, fiancée without consolation,
I see you between cliffs and hurricanes
as wide and lonely as the sky.

Heart of lightning and eagerness,
paging the books of your roses,
feeding the herd of your breads.

You were going to be the flower of wives,
and between flashes of lightning your husband
fades from you with flour-caked hands.

Cast flour, you clamorous black bull,
until the point where your slight
woolly fleece grows white and quiet.

I help you to throw flakes of flour
and to suffer below it, my companion,
widow of the body, and I, widower of the soul.

Implacable death waits for us
like an incessant, miscarried water
surrounding each glass window.

¡Cuántos amargos tragos es la vida!
Bebió él la muerte y tú la saboreas
y yo no saboreo otra bebida.

Retírate conmigo hasta que veas
con nuestro llanto dar las piedras grama,
abandonando el pan que pastoreas.

Levántate: te esperan tus zapatos
junto a los suyos muertos en tu cama,
y la lluviaosa pena en sus retratos
desde cuyos presidios te reclama.

How many bitter drinks is life!
He drank death and you savor it
and I do not savor another drink.

Retreat with me until you see
with our tears to give the stones grass,
leaving the bread that you shepherd.

Awaken: your shoes wait for you
together like all those dead in your bed,
and the rain-streaked pain in his portrait
is a prison from which he calls to you.

TED GENOWAYS

Me empuje a martillazados y mordiscos,
me tira con bramidas y cordeles
del corazón, del pie, de los orígenes,
me clava en la garganta garfios dulces,
erizo entre mis dedos y mis ojos,
enloquece mis uñas y mis párpados,
rodea mis palabras y mi alcoba
de hornos y herrerías,
la dirección altera de mi lengua,
y sembrando de cera su camino
hace que caiga torpe derretida.

Mujer, mira una sangre,
mira una blusa de azafrán en celo,
mira un capote líquido ciñéndose en mis huesos
como descomunales serpientes que me oprimen
acarreando angustia por mis venas.

Mira una fuente alzada de amorosos collares
y cencerros de voz atribulada
temblando de impaciencia por ocupar tu cuello,
un dictamen feroz, una sentencia
una exigencia, una dolencia, un río
que por manifestarse se da contra las piedras,
y penden para siempre de mis
relicarios de carne desgarrada.

Mírala con sus chivos y sus toros suicidas
corneando cabestros y montañas,
rompiéndose los cuernos a topazos,
mordiéndose de rabia las orejas,
buscándose la muerte de la frente a la cola.

Manejando mi sangre, enarbolando
revoluciones de carbón y yodo,
agrupando hasta hacerse corazón,
herramientas de muerte, rayos, hachas,

It prods me with bites and hammer-blows,
tugs me with bellows by the cords
of my heart, of my feet, of my ancestry,
nails my throat with its sweet meat-hooks,
like a thistle between my fingers and my eyes,
enraging my nails and my lids,
wrapping my words and my bedroom
in ovens and iron forges,
their direction altered by my tongue,
sowing its road with wax
that has fallen dumb and melted.

Woman, behold my blood,
behold a saffron blouse in rutting-heat,
behold a liquid cloak twisted around my bones
like uncommon serpents that oppress me
carrying anguish through my veins.

Behold an upraised fountain of loving necklaces
and cowbells with plaintive voices
trembling with impatience to occupy your neck,
a fierce dictate, a sentence,
a demand, an ache, a river
that throws itself against the rocks,
forever hanging over my
reliquaries of rended flesh.

Behold it with its rams and suicidal bulls
butting halters and mountains,
horns breaking on impact,
biting its ears in anger,
seeking death from head to tail.

Managing my blood hoisting
revolutions of cinder and iodine
clustered until it takes heart,
ironworks of death, lightning bolts, hatchets,

y barrancos de espuma sin apoyo,
ando pidiendo un cuerpo que manchar.

Hazte cargo, hazte cargo
de una ganadería de alacranes
tan rencorosamente enamorados,
de un castigo infinito que me parió y me agobia
como un jornal cobrado en triste plomo.

La puerta de mi sangre está en la esquina
del hacha y de la piedra,
pero en ti está la entrada irremediable.

Necesito extender este imperioso reino,
prolongar a mis padres hasta la eternidad,
y tiendo hacia ti un puente de arqueados corazones
que ya se corrompieron y que aún laten.

No me pongas obstáculos que tengo que salvar,
no me siembres de cárceles,
no bastan cerraduras ni cementos,
no, a encadenar mi sangre de alquitrán inflamado
capaz de despertar calentura en la nieve.

¡Ay qué ganas de amarte contra un árbol,
ay qué afán de trillarte en una era,
ay qué dolor de verte por la espalda
y no verte la espalda contra el mundo!

Mi sangre es un camino ante el crepúsculo
de apasionado barro y charcos vaporosos
que tiene que acabar en tus entrañas,
un depósito mágico de anillos
que ajustar a tu sangre,
un sembrado de lunas eclipsadas
que han de aumentar sus calabazas íntimas
ahogadas en un vino con canas en los labios,
al pie de tu cintura al fin sonora.

and ravines of spume without fulcrum,
walking, craving a body to corrupt.

Take upon yourself, take upon yourself
a stock-pen of scorpions,
so rancorously lovestruck,
an infinite punishment that bends me and that I bear
like day-labor received in a sad bullet.

The door to my blood is on the corner
between the axe and the stone,
but in you lies the irremediable entry.

I must extend this imperious reign,
prolong my fathers until eternity,
and I stretch out toward you a bridge of retching hearts
which are already decayed and which still beat.

Don't throw up any obstacles for me to clear,
don't sow my way with prisons,
neither locks nor cement are enough,
no, to shackle this blood like burning pitch
capable of waking a fever from the snow.

Oh, how I burn to love you against a tree,
how eagerly I would thresh you,
what pain to see you from behind
and not see your back to the world!

My blood is a road before the twilight
of impassioned mud and steamy puddles
which must end in you,
a magical deposit of rings
to adjust to your blood,
a field of eclipsed moons
that has to enlarge its intimate gourds
drowned in a wine with white hairs on its lips,
near to your waist which at last sings.

Guárdame de sus sombras que graznan fatalmente
girando en torno mío a picotazos,
girasoles de cuervos borrascosos.
No me consientas ir de sangre en sangre
como una bala loca,
no me dejes tronar solo y tendido.

Pólvora venenosa propagada,
ornado por los ojos de tristes pirotecnias,
panal horriblemente acribillado
como un mínimo rayo doliendo en cada poro,
gremio fosforescente de acechantes tarántulas
no me consientas ser. Atiende, atiende
a mi desesperado sonreír,
donde muerdo la hiel por sus raíces
por las lluviosas penas recorrido.
Recibe esta fortuna sedienta de tu boca
que para ti heredé de tanto padre.

Save me from the shadows which caw fatefully
wheeling about me and pecking,
turning like sunflowers of stormy crows.
Don't allow me to go blood on blood
like a stray bullet,
don't leave me to thunder, alone and cast away.

Venomous, propagated gunpowder,
ornamented by the eyes of sad fireworks,
honeycomb horribly riddled with holes
by a small lightning bolt aching in every pore,
don't allow me to be a phosphorescent cluster
of ambushing tarantulas. Attend, attend
to my desperate smile,
where I tear bitterness from its roots
by floods of recurrent sorrows.
Receive this fate thirsting for your mouth
which I inherited for you from so many ancestors.

TED GENOWAYS

Patio de vecindad que nadie alquila
igual que un pueblo de panales secos;
pintadas con recuerdos y leche las paredes
a mi ventana emiten silencios y anteojos.

Aquí dentro: aquí anduvo la muerte mi vecina
sesteando a la sombra de los spultuereros,
lamida por la lengua de un perro guarda-lápidas;
aquí, muy preservados del relente y las penas,
porfiaron los muertos con los muertos
rivalizando en huesos como en mármoles.

Oigo una voz de rostro desmayado,
unos cuervos que informan mi corazón de luto
haciéndome tragar húmedas ranas,
echándome a la cara los tornasoles trémulos
que devuelve en su espejo la inquietud.

¿Qué queda en este campo secuestrado.
en estas minas de carbón y plomo,
de tantos encerrados por riguroso orden?

No hay nada sin un monte de riqueza explotado.
Los enterrados con bastón y mitra,
los altos personajes de la muerte,
las niñas que expiraron de sed por la entrepierna
donde jamás tuvieron un arado y dos bueyes,
los duros picadores pródigos de sus músculos,
muertos con las heridas rodeadas de cuernos:
todos los destetados del aire y del amor
de un polvo huésped ahora se amamantan.

¿Y para quién están los tiernos epitafios,
las alabanzas más sañudas,
formulades a fuerza de cincel y mentiras,
atacando el silencio natural de las piedras,
todas con menoscabos y agujeros

Neighborhood patio that nobody rents
like a town of arid honeycombs,
adorned with memories and shit, the walls
exude silence and blinkers for my sight.

Within, here walked my neighbor Death
resting in the shadow of gravediggers,
fawned upon by a servile guardian of tombs,
here, well protected from the dew and worries
the dead argue obstinately among themselves
competing in their bones as in their memorials.

I hear a voice of funereal tone,
some crows that inform my grieving heart
making me swallow obscenities,
flinging in my face uncertain illusions
which anxiety reflects in its mirror.

What remains of this sequestered field,
in these mines of coal and lead,
of so many imprisoned by inexorable order?

There is nothing without an exploited hill of wealth.
Those buried with crook and mitre,
the aristocracy of death,
those girls who died of arid chastity
whose thighs never knew the plough,
the harshly lavish thrusts of the picador's goad,
corpses with wounds surrounded by horns,
all those deprived of air and love
are suckled now with lodging-house dust.

For whom are the loving epitaphs,
the merciless eulogies
expressed so strongly with chisel and lies,
attacking the natural silence of the gravestones,
all with blemishes and holes

de ser ramoneadas con hambre y con constancia
por una amante oveja de dos labios?
¿Y este espolón constituido en gallo
irá a una sombra malgastada en mármol y ladrillo?
¿No cumplirá mi sangre su misión: ser estiércol?
¿Oiré cómo murmuran de mis huesos,
me mirarán con esa mirada de tinaja vacía
que de la muerte a todo el que la trata?
¿Me asaltarán espectros en forma de cornonas,
funerarios nacidos del pecado
de un cirio y una caja boquiabierta?

Yo no quiero agregar pechuga al polvo:
me niego a su destino: ser echado a un rincón.
Prefiero que me coman los lobos y los perros,
que mis huesos actúen como estacas
para atar cerdos o picar espartos.

El polvo es paz llega con su bandera blanca
sobre los ataúdes y las casas caídas,
pero bajo los pliegues un colmillo
de rabioso marfil contaminado
nos sigue a todas partes, nos vigila,
y apenas nos paramos nos inciensa de siglos,
nos reduce a cornisas y a santos arrumbados.

Y es que el polvo no es tierra.

La tierra es un amor dispuesto a ser un hoyo,
dispuesto a ser un árbol, un volcán y una fuente.

Mi cuerpo pide el hoyo que promete la tierra,
el hoyo desde el cual daré mis privilegios de léon y nitrato
a todas las raíces que me tiendan sus trenzas.

Guárdate de que el polvo coloque dulcemente
su secular paloma en tu cabeza,
de que incube sus huevos en tus labios,
de que anide cayédose en tus ojos,

from being hungrily and constantly browsed
by a two-lipped loving sheep?
And will this buttress made into ridge-poles
become a squandered shade in marble and stone?
Won't my blood complete its mission, become manure?
Will I hear how they speak of my bones,
will they regard me with that gaze of an empty jar
which death gives to those acquainted with it?
Will ghosts shaped like wreaths attack me,
funerals born of the sin
of a candle and gaping coffin?

I don't want to add my breast to the dust.
I decline its fate, to be flung in a corner.
I'd rather the wolves and dogs eat me,
that my bones are used as stakes
to tie up swine or pierce esparto.

Dust is a peace that drapes its white flag
over coffins and bereaved houses,
but beneath the folds a fang
of corrupt and furious ivory
pursues us everywhere, watches us,
and no sooner do we stop flatters us with centuries,
reducing us to cornices and saintly neglect.

Dust is not earth.

Earth is a love prepared to become a grave,
ready to be a tree, a volcano, and a stream.

My body asks for the grave that earth promises,
the hole from which I'll give my store of lion and nitrate
to all the roots that stretch out their tresses to me.

Watch out lest the dust gently lay
its secular dove on your head,
lest it hatch its eggs on your lips
and build its nest falling into your eyes

de que habite tranquilo en tu vestido,
de aceptar sus herencias de notarios y templos.

Usate en contra suya,
defiéndete de su callado ataque,
asústalo con besos y caricias,
ahuyéntalo con saltos y canciones,
mátalo rociándolo de vino, amor y sangre.

En esta gran bodega donde fermenta el polvo,
donde es inútil injerir sonrisas,
pido ser cuando quieto lo que no soy movido:
un vegetal, sin ojos ni problemas;
cuajar, cuajar en algo más que en polvo,
como el sueño en estatua derribada;
que mis zapatos últimos demuestren ser cortezas,
que me produzcan cuarzos en mi encantada boca,
que se apoyen en mí sembrados y viñedos,
que me dediquen mosto las cepas por su orige.

Aquel barbecho lleno de inagotables besos,
aquella cesta de uvas quiero tener encima
cuando descanse al fin de esta faena
de dar conversaciones, abrazos y pesares,
de cultivar cabellos, arrugas y esperanzas,
y de sentir un beso sobre cada deseo.

No quiero que me entierren donde me han de enterrar.
Haré un hoyo en el campo y esperaré a que venga
la muerte en dirección a mi garganta
con un cuerno, un tintero, un monaguillo
y un collar de cencerros castrados en la lengua,
para echarme puñados de mi especie.

or live quietly in your clothing
through accepting its heritage of scribes and churches.

Set yourself in opposition,
defend yourself from its silent attack,
frighten it away with kisses and caresses,
drive it off with songs and dancing,
kill it by spraying it with wine, love, and blood.

In that great cellar where dust ferments,
where it's useless to let in smiles,
I ask to be left undisturbed and at rest,
a vegetable without eyes or problems,
to congeal, curdle into something more than dust,
like the dream in the demolished statue,
that my last shoes may prove to be bark,
may bear me quartzes in my gratified mouth,
that grainfields and vineyards may depend on me,
and vines honor me with their juice.

That fallow filled with inexhaustible kisses,
that basket of grapes I wish to have above me
when I rest at the end of this toil
of talk, embraces, and sorrows,
of cultivating hair, wrinkles, and hopes,
and of feeling a kiss upon each desire.

I don't want them to bury me where they have to.
I'll dig a grave in the fields and wait
for death's approach in my throat
with a horn, an inkwell, an acolyte
and a collar of iron bells with castrated tongues
to fling me handfuls of my kind.

GEOFFREY HOLIDAY

Vengo muy satisfecho de librarme
de la serpiente de las múltiples cúpulas,
la serpiente escamada de casullas y cálices:
su cola puso acíbar en mi boca, sus anillos verdugos
reprimieron y malaventuraron la nudosa sangre de mi
    corazón.
Vengo muy dolorido de aquel infierno de incensarios
    locos,
de aquella boba gloria: sonreídme.

Sonreídme, que voy
a donde estáis vosotros los de siempre,
los que cubrís de espigas y racimos la boca del que os
    escupe,
los que conmigo en surcos, andamios, fraguas, hornos,
os arrancáis la corona de sudor a diario.

Me libré de los templos: sonreídme,
donde me consumía con tristeza de lámpara
encerrado en el poco aire de los sagrarios.
Salte al monte de donde procedo,
a las viñas donde halla tanta hermana mi sangre,
a vuestra compañía de relativo barro.

Agrupo mi hambre, mis penas y estas cicatrices
que llevo de tratar piedras y hachas
a vuestras hambres, vuestras penas y vuestra herrada
    carne,
porque para calmar nuestra desesperación de toros
    castigados
habemos de agruparnos oceánicamente.

Nubes tempestuosas de herramientas
para un cielo de manos vengativas
nos es preciso. Ya relampaguean
las hachas y las hoces con su metal crispado,
ya truenan los martillos y los mazos

I am very satisfied that I have freed myself
from the serpent of multiple cupolas,
the serpent scaled with vestments and chalices:
its tail filled my mouth with bitterness, its executioner
    rings
repressed and brought grief to the knotty blood of my
    heart.
I come greatly pained from that inferno of burning
    madmen,
from that glorious fool: smile at me.

Smile at me, because I am going
to the place where you, the usual ones, are,
you who cover the mouth of one who spits on you with
    grain and grape clusters,
you who with me in the furrows, scaffolds, smithies, blast
    furnaces,
wrest from yourselves a crown of sweat each day.

I freed myself from the temples: smile at me,
where I would be consumed by the sadness of a lamp
enclosed in the little air of those sanctuaries.
I leapt up to the mountain from which I came,
to the vineyards where my blood finds its brothers,
to your company of kindred clay.

I gather my hunger, my sorrows, and these scars
that I wear from my working with stones and axes,
to your hungers, your sorrows, and your branded flesh,
because to calm our desperation of castigated bulls
we have to come together into an oceanic roar.

Tempestuous clouds of ironworks
for a sky of vengeful hands
are necessary. Already they illuminate
the hatchets and the sickles with their shriveled metal,
already the hammers and the mallets thunder

sobre los pensamientos de los que nos han hecho
burros de carga y bueyes de labor.
Salta el capitalista de su cochino lujo,
huyen los arzobispos de sus mitras obscenas,
los notarios y los registradores de la propiedad
caen aplastados bajo furiosos protocolos,
los curas se deciden a ser hombres
y abierta ya la jaula donde actúa el león
queda el oro en la más espantosa miseria.

En vuestros puños quiero ver rayos contrayéndose,
quiero ver a la cólera tirándoos de las cejas,
la cólera me nubla todas las cosas dentro del corazón
sintiendo el martillazo del hambre en el ombligo,
viendo a mi hermana helarse mientras lava la ropa,
viendo a mi madre siempre en ayuno forzoso,
viéndoos en este estado capaz de impacientar
a los mismos corderos que jamás se impacientan.

Habrá que ver la tierra estercolada con las injustas
    sangres,
habrá que ver la media vuelta fiera de la hoz ajustándose
    a las nucas,
habrá que verlo todo noblemente impasibles,
habrá que hacerlo todo sufriendo un poco menos de lo
    que ahora sufrimos bajo el hambre,
que nos hace alargar las inocentes manos animales
hacia el robo y el crimen salvadores.

over the thoughts of those who have turned us into beasts
    of burden.
The capitalist leaps from his dirty extravagance,
archbishops escape from their obscene mitres,
the notaries and the registrars of property
fall flattened under furious protocols,
the priests decide to be men
and in the already-open cage where the lion performs
remains the gold in its most horrible misery.

In your fists I want to see lightning bolts flash,
I want to see bile pulling your eyebrows,
bile clouds over everything in my heart
feeling hunger's hammer-strike in my belly,
seeing my sister ice over while washing clothes,
seeing my mother ever forced to fast,
seeing you in this state could irritate
those same lambs that never lose their impatience.

We will have to see the fields fertilized with wrongful
    blood,
We will have to see the fierce crescent of the sickle
    approaching the napes,
We will have to see it all nobly impassive,
We will have to do it all suffering a little less than what we
    suffer now from hunger,
that makes us reach out our innocent animal hands
toward robbery and crime, our saviors.

TED GENOWAYS

Amanecen las hachas en bandadas
como ganaderías voladoras
de laboriosas grullas combatientes.

Las alas son relámpagos cuajados,
las plumas, puños, muertes las canciones,
el aire en que se apoyan para el vuelo
brazos que gesticulan como rayos.

Amanecen las hachas destruyendo y cantando.

Se cubren las cabezas de peligros
y amenazas mortales:
temen los asesinos que preservan cañones,
los órganos se callan a torrentes
y Dios desaparece del Sagrario
envuelto en telarañas seculares.

Vuela un presentimiento de heridas sobre todos,
llega una tempestad atronadora
de ceños como yugos peligrosos.
Se aproximan miradas catastróficas,
pies desbocados, manos encrespadas,
hachas amanecidas goteando relente.

Vienen talando, golpeando, ansiando
asustan corazones de rapiña,
ahuyentan cuervos de podrido vuelo,
y el ruido de sus bruscos aletazos
hace palidecer al mismo oro.

Donde posan su vuelo revientan sangre y savia
como densas bebidas animales,
donde canta su ira alza el espanto
su cabello de pronto encanecido,
donde sus picotazos se encarnizan
se apagan corazones como brasas echadas en un pozo

The hatchets dawn in coveys
like flying stock-pens
of toilsome, combatant cranes.

Their wings are ornate flashes of lightning,
their feathers, fists, death their song;
the air which supports them in flight,
arms that gesture like bolts of lightning.

The hatchets dawn destroying and singing.

They cover their heads with perils
and mortal threats:
they fear assassins who guard cannons,
torrents of organs are silenced
and God disappears from the sanctuary
wrapped in secular cobwebs.

A premonition of wounds flies over everyone,
a frowning thundering tempest
arrives like perilous yokes.
Catastrophic gazes come near,
wild feet, curled hands,
dawning hatchets dripping with dew.

They come felling, pounding, yearning
they frighten pillaging hearts,
drive away crows with rotten flight,
and the noise of their rough wingbeats
makes even gold turn pale.

Where they perch, blood and sap break loose
like thick animal drinks,
where their ire sings, fear mounts,
its hairs, suddenly graying,
where their beaks are glutted with flesh,
they quench hearts like live coals cast in a well,

donde su dentadura dura muerde
hay grandes cataclismos de todas las especies.

Ferozmente risueñas, entre manos
igual que remos, hachas iracundas,
voces de un solo hachazo,
truenos de un seco y único bramido
y relámpagos de hojas repentinas,
talan las hachas bosques y conventos,
tumban las hachas troncos y palacios
que tienen por entrañas carcoma y yesca estéril,
y caen brazos y ramas confundidos,
nidadas, sombras, pomas y cabezas
en un derrumbamiento babilónico.

Amanecen las hachas crispadas, vengativas.
Sacuden las serpientes su látigo asustado
de su expresión mortal de rayo rudo.

Con nuestra catadura de hachas nuevas,
¡a las aladas hachas, compañeros,
sobre los viejos troncos carcomidos!
Que nos teman, que se echen al cuello las raíces
y se ahorquen, que vamos, que venimos,
jornaleros del árbol, leñadores.

where their teeth bite down,
there are grand cataclysms of all kinds.

Ferociously smiling, between hands
that labor equally, furious hatchets,
voices of a solitary ax-stroke,
thunderings of a dry and singular roar
and lightning flashes of sudden leaves,
hatchets that destroy forests and convents,
the hatchets topple trunks and palaces
that have wood lice and barren tinder for entrails.
arms and puzzled branches fall,
nests, shelters, apples, and heads
in a Babylonian collapse.

The hatchets dawn shriveled, vengeful.
Serpents shake their whips frightened
of their deadly expression of a harsh shaft of light.

With our appearance of new hatchets,
with hatchets like fluttering wings, comrades,
take to the old, louse-eaten trunks!
May they fear us, may the roots coil round their necks
and hang them, because we go, we come,
journeymen to the tree, woodsmen.

TED GENOWAYS

De sangre en sangre vengo,
como el mar de ola en ola,
de color de amapola el alma tengo,
de amapola sin suerte es mi destino,
y llego de amapola en amapola
a dar en la cornada de mi sino.

Criatura hubo que vino
desde la sementera de la nada,
y vino más de una
bajo el designio de una estrella aireada
en una turbulenta y mala luna.

Cayó una pincelada
de ensangrantado pie sobre mi herida,
cayó un planeta de azafrán en celo,
cayó una nube roja enfurecida,
cayó un mar malherido, cayó un cielo.

Vine con un dolor de cuchillada
me esperaba un cuchillo en mi venida,
me dieron a mamar leche de tuera,
zumo de espada loca y homicida,
y al sol el ojo abrí por vez primera
y lo que vi primero era una herida
y una desgracia era.

Me persigue la sangre ávida y fiera,
desde que fuí fundado,
y aún antes de que fuera
proferido, empujado
por mi madre a esta tierra codiciosa
que de los pies me tira y del costado,
y cada vez más fuerte hacia la fosa.

Lucho contra la sangre, me debato
contra tanto zarpazo y tanta vena

I come, blood on blood,
like the sea, wave on wave.
I have a soul the color of poppies.
The luckless poppy is my destiny,
from poppy to poppy I come
to fall on the horns of my fate.

A creature must grow
from the seedbed of nothing,
and more than one turns up
under the design of an angry star,
under a troubled and bad moon.

The brushstroke
of a bloodstained foot fell over my wound,
a planet of fired-up saffron fell,
an enraged red cloud fell,
a badly wounded ocean fell, a sky.

I came with the knife's pain,
a knife was waiting when I got here.
They suckled me on the milk of the bitterapple,
the juice of a crazy, murderous blade,
and when my eye opened to the sun for the first time
the first thing I saw was a wound,
and that was bad luck.

Vivid, ferocious flood, which formed me,
and chases me down.
Before I even had a name
my mother shoved me into this ravening land,
threw me onto my feet, and onto my side,
pushed me harder each time, toward the grave.

I fight with blood, I argue
with the pounding of bodies, with all those veins,

y cada cuerpo que tropiezo y trato
es otro borbotón de sangre, otra cadena

Aunque leves los dardos de la pena
aumentan las insignias de mi pecho:
en él se dió el amor a la labranza,
y mi alma de barbecho
hodamente ha surcado
de heridas sin remedio mi esperanza
por las ansias de muerte de su arado.

Todas las herramientas en mi acecho:
recónditas señales,
las piedras, los deseos y los días
cavaron en mi cuerpo manantiales
que sólo se tragaron las arenas
y las melancolías.

Son cada vez más grandes las cadena,
son cada vez mas grandes las serpientes,
más grande y más cruel su poderío,
más grandes sus anillos envolventes,
más grande el corazón, más grande el mío.

En su alcoba poblada de vacío
donde sólo concurren las visitas,
el picotazo y el dolor de un cuervo,
un manojo de cartas y pasiones escritas,
un puñado de sangre y una muerte conservo.

¡Ay sangre fulminante,
ay trepadora púrpura regiente,
sentencia a todas horas resonante
bajo el yunque sufrido de mi frente!

La sangre me ha parido y me ha hecho preso,
la sangre me reduce y me agiganta,
un edificio soy de sangre y yeso

and each body I bump into and contend with
is one more cauldron of blood, one more chain.

Though they are light, barbs of pain
mount up like badges on my chest:
That's where love of farming wounds me,
and my deeply fallowed soul
has furrowed my hope with untreatable wounds
from the death agony of its plough.

All the implements
lie in wait for me: the hatchet has left
secret signs for me,
stones, desires, and days
have excavated wellsprings inside my body
which, by themselves, swallow up sand
and melancholy.

The chains get stronger each time,
the snakes get stronger each time,
its power is greater and crueler,
the enveloping rings stronger, stronger
the heart, my heart.

In its vacuum-thick domicile—
the only place these visitations occur—
I keep a handful of letters and inscribed passions,
a jot of blood, and death.

Ay, frothing blood,
ay, roaring purple climber,
verdict on all the hours resounding
from beneath my head's long-suffering anvil!

Blood has given me birth, and jail.
Blood dissolves me and swells me up.
I am a building constructed of blood and plaster

que se derriba él mismo y se levanta
sobre andamios de huesos.

Un albañil de sangre, muerto y rojo,
llueve y cuelga su blusa cada día
en los alrededores de mi ojo,
y cada noche con el alma mía
y hasta con las pestañas lo recojo.

Crece la sangre, agranda
la expansión de sus frondas en mi pecho
que álamo desbordante se desmanda
y en varios torvos ríos cae deshecho.

Me veo de repente
envuelto en sus coléricos raudales,
y nado contra todos desesperadamente
como contra un fatal torrente de puñales.

Me arrastra encarnizada su corriente,
me despedaza, me hunde, me atropella,
quiero apartarme de ella a manotazos,
y se me van los brazos detrás de ella,
y se me van las ansias en los brazos.

Me dejaré arrastrar hecho pedazos,
ya que así se lo ordenan a mi vida
la sangre y su marea,
los cuerpos y mi estrella ensangrentada.

Seré una sola y dilatada herida
hasta que dilatadamente sea
un cadáver de espuma: viento y nada.

which demolishes and rebuilds itself
on a bone scaffolding.

A bricklayer in blood, dying blood,
washes and hangs out his shirt each day
not far from my eye,
and each night, with my soul,
and even with my eyelids, I gather it all back in.

Blood blooms, spreads
its wide foliage in my chest,
its brimming poplar grows wild
and falls violently undone into several fierce rivers.

Suddenly I see
that I am drowning in its angry torrents,
and I swim desperately against them
as if against a lethal stream of daggers.

The current drags me till it is glutted,
it tears me to pieces, sinks me, tramples me.
I wish I could haul myself away from its blows,
hoist my arms out of it,
draw the pain from my arms.

It will quit dragging me to pieces,
now that it ordains my life,
blood and its tide,
bodies, my bloody star.

I will be one dilated wound,
distended till there is
a corpse of foam: wind and nothing.

DON SHARE

147

Hoy estoy sin saber yo no sé cómo,
hoy estoy para penas solamente,
hoy no tengo amistad,
hoy sólo tengo ansias
de arrancarme de cuajo el corazón
y ponerlo debajo de un zapato.

Hoy reverdece aquella espina seca,
hoy es día de llantos en mi reino,
hoy descarga en mi pecho el desaliento
plomo desalentado.

No puedo con mi estrella.
Y me busco la muerte por las manos
mirando con cariño las navajas,
y recuerdo aquel hacha compañera,
y pienso en los mas altos campanarios
para un salto mortal serenamente.

Si no fuera ¿por qué? . . . no sé por qué,
mi corazón escribiria una postrera carta,
una carta que llevo aquí metida,
haría un tintero de mi corazón,
una fuente de sílabas, de adioses y regalos,
y ahí te quedas, al mundo le diría.

Yo nací en mala luna.
Tengo la pena de una sola pena
que vale mas que toda la alegría.
Un amor me ha dejado con los brazos caídos
y no puedo tenderlos hacia más.
¿No veis mi boca qué desengañada,
que incorformes mis ojos?

Cuanto más me contemplo más me aflijo:
cortar este dolor ¿con qué tijeras?

Today I am, I don't know how,
today all I am ready for is suffering,
today I have no friends,
today the only thing I have is the desire
to rip out my heart by the roots
and stick it underneath a shoe.

Today that dry thorn is growing strong again,
today is the day of crying in my kingdom,
depression unloads today in my chest
a depressed heavy metal.

Today my destiny is too much for me.
And I'm looking for death down by my hands,
looking at knives with affection,
and I remember that friendly ax,
and all I think about is the tallest steeples
and making a fatal leap serenely.

If it weren't for . . . I don't know what,
my heart would write a suicide note,
a note I carry hidden there,
I would make an inkwell out of my heart,
a fountain of syllables, and good-byes and gifts,
and you stay here I'd say to the world.

I was born under a rotten star.
My grief is that I only have one grief
and it weighs more than all the joys together.
A love affair has left me with my arms hanging down
and I can't lift them anymore.
Don't you see how disillusioned my mouth is?
How unsatisfied my eyes are?

The more I look inward the more I mourn!
Cut off this pain?—who has the scissors?

Ayer, mañana, hoy
padeciendo por todo
mi corazón, pecera melancólica,
penal de ruiseñores moribundos.

Me sobra corazón.

Hoy descorazonarme,
yo el más corazonado de los hombres,
y por el más, también el más amargo.

No sé por qué, no sé por qué no cómo
me perdono la vida cada día.

Yesterday, tomorrow, today
suffering for everything,
my heart is a sad goldfish bowl,
a pen of dying nightingales.

I have plenty of heart.

Today to rip out my heart,
I who have a bigger heart than anyone,
and having that, I am the bitterest also.

I don't know why, I don't know how or why
I let my life keep on going every day.

ROBERT BLY

EL VIENTO DEL PUEBLO
(1937)

WIND OF THE PEOPLE

(1937)

Vicente: A nosotros, que hemos nacido poetas entre todos los hombres, nos ha hecho poetas la vida junto a todos los hombres. Nosotros venimos brotando del manantial de las guit arras acogidas por el pueblo, y cada poeta que muere deja en manos de otro, como una herencia, un instrumento que viene rodando desde la eternidad de la nada a nuestro corazón esparcido. Ante la sombra de dos poetas, nos levantamos otros dos, y ante la nuestra se levantarán otros dos de mañana. Nuestro cimiento será siempre el mismo: la tierra. Nuestro destino es parar en las manos del pueblo. Sólo esas honradas manos pueden contener lo que la sangre honrada del poeta derrama vibrante. Aquel que se atreve a manchar esas manos, aquellos que se atreven a deshonrar esa sangre, son los traidores asesinos del pueblo y la poesía, y nadie los lavará: en su mismo venero. Lo que echo de menos en mi guitarra, lo hallo en la tuya. Pablo Neruda y tu me habéis dado imborrable pruebas de poesía, y el pueblo hacia el que tiendo todas mis raíces alimenta y ensancha mis ansias y mis cuerdas con el soplo cálido de sus movimientos nobles.

Los poetas somos viento del pueblo: nacemos para pasar soplando a través de sus poros y conducir sus ojos y sus sentimientos hacia la cumbres más hermosas. Hoy, este hoy de pasión, de vi da, de muerte, nos empuja de un imponente modo a ti, a mí, a varios, hacia el pueblo. El pueblo espera a los poetas con la oreja y el alma tendidas al pie de cada siglo.

I DEDICATE THIS BOOK
TO VICENTE ALEIXANDRE

Vicente: To us, who of all men have been born poets, whom life has made poets among men. We come from the spring of the guitars welcomed by the people, and each poet who dies leaves in the hands of another, like an inheritance, an instrument that comes rolling from the eternity of nothingness to our scattered heart. Under the shade of two poets, we rose we two, and under ours two others will rise tomorrow. Our foundation will be always the same: the earth. Our destiny is to end up in the hands of the people. Only those honest hands can contain what the honest blood of the vibrant poet spills. Those who dare to stain those hands, those who dare to dishonor that blood, are the treasonous assassins of the people and poetry, and nobody will wash them clean: in the same spring water. What I miss in my guitar, I find it in yours. Pablo Neruda and you have given me indelible tastes of poetry, and the people for whom I offer all my roots feed and widen my anxieties and my sensibility with the warm breath of their noble movements.

We poets are the wind of the people: we are born to go blowing through their pores and to lead their eyes and their feelings toward the most beautiful summits. Today, this day of passion, of life, of death, pushes us, you, me, and others, down in an imposing way, toward the people. The people wait for the poets with attentive ears and souls spread wide at the foot of each century.

TED GENOWAYS

ELEGÍA PRIMERA

A Federico García Lorca, poeta

Atraviesa la muerte con herrumbrosas lanzas,
y en traje de cañón, las parameras
donde cultiva el hombre raíces y esperanzas,
y llueve sal, y esparce calaveras.

Verdura de las eras,
¿qué tiempo prevalece la alegría?
El sol pudre la sangre, la cubre de asechanzas
y hace brotar la sombra más sombría.

El dolor y su manto
vienen una vez más a nuestro encuentro.
Y una vez más al callejón del llanto
lluviosamente entro.

Siempre me veo dentro
de esta sombra de acíbar revocada
amasado con ojos y bordones,
que un candil de agonía tiene puesto a la entrada
y un rabioso collar de carazones.

Llorar dentro de un pozo,
en la misma raíz desconsalada
del agua, del sollozo,
del corazón quisiera;
donde nadie me viera la voz ni la mirada,
ni restos de mis lágrimas me viera.

Entro despacio, se me cae la frente
despacio, el corazón se me desgarra
despacio, y despaciosa y negramente
vuelvo a llorar al pie de una guitarra.

Entre todos los muertos de elegía,
sin olvidar el eco de ninguno,

for Federico García Lorca, poet

Death crosses through fields with rusty spears,
and clad in cannons, the moorlands
where man cultivates roots and hopes,
and showers salt, and scatters skulls.

Fruit of the gardens,
what weather rules happiness?
The sun rots the blood, covers it with snares
and makes the shadows more somber.

Pain and its silk veil
come once more to meet us.
And once more into the narrow pass
of tears, I enter rain-soaked.

I always see myself within
this shadow of revoked bitterness
molded by eyes and sticks,
which a candle of agony has placed at the entrance
and a furious necklace of hearts.

I would like to weep within a well,
in the same disconsolate hole
of water, of sobs,
of the longing heart:
where nobody would hear my voice
nor the reflection, nor the rest of my tears.

I enter slowly, I bow my head
slowly, I rend my heart
slowly, and slowly and blackly
I weep again at the feet of a guitar.

Among all the dead in elegies,
not forgetting the echo of any,

por haber resonado más en el alma mía,
la mano de mi llanto escoge uno.

Federico García
hasta ayer se llamó: polvo se llama.
Ayer tuvo un espacio bajo el día
que hoy el hoyo le da bajo la grama.

¡Tanto fue! ¡Tanto fuiste y ya no eres!
Tu agitada alegría,
que agitaba columnas y alfileres,
de tus dientes arrancas y sacudes,
y ya te pones triste, y sólo quieres
ya el paraíso de los ataúdes.
Vestido de esqueleto,
durmiéndote de plomo,
de indiferencia armado y de respeto,
te veo entre tus cejas si me asomo.

Se ha llevado tu vida de palomo,
que ceñía de espuma
y de arrullos el cielo y las ventanas
como un raudal de pluma
el viento que se lleva las semanas.

Primo de las manzanas,
no podrá con tu savia la carcoma,
no podrá con tu muerte la lengua del gusano,
y para dar de salud fiera a su poma
elegirá tus huesos el manzano.

Cegado el manantial de tu saliva,
hijo de la paloma,
nieto del ruiseñor y de la oliva:
serás, mientras la tierra vaya y vuelva,
esposo siempre de la siempreviva,
estiércol padre de la madreselva.

my tear-stained hand chooses one
that has resonated most in my soul.

Until yesterday he was called
Federico García: now he is called dust.
Yesterday he had a place under the sun
but today he is put in a hole under the grass.

He was so much! You were so much and are no more!
Your stirring joy,
that stirred columns and rows
with your teeth you uproot and shake,
and become sad, and you want
only the paradise of coffins.
If I peek out, I see you between your brows,
I see you dressed as a skeleton,
dreaming of a lead bullet,
armed with indifference and with respect.

The wind that takes away the weeks
has taken away your pigeon-life,
and surrounded the sky with spume
and with cooing and the windows
like a streaming plume.

Cousin to the apples,
the louse can't prune your sap
the maggot's tongue can't prune your death,
and to give your apple scent fierce health
the apple tree will choose your bones.

Son of the dove,
grandson of the nightingale and the olive:
though the spring of your saliva be filled in,
you will be, while the earth goes and returns,
husband always of the immortelle,
dung-father of the honeysuckle.

¡Qué sencilla es la muerte: qué sencilla,
pero qué injustamente arrebatada!
No sabe andar despacio, y acuchilla
cuando menos se espera tu turbia cuchillada.

Tú, el más firme edificio, destruido,
tú, el gavilán más alto, desplomado,
tú, el más grande rugido,
callado, y más callado, y más callado.

Caiga tu alegre sangre de granado,
como un derrumbamiento de martillos feroces,
sobre quién te detuvo mortalmente.
Salivazos y hoces
caigan sobre la mancha de su frente.

Muere un poeta y la creación se siente
herida y moribunda en las entrañas.
Un cósmico temblor de escalofríos
mueve temiblemente las montañas,
un resplandor de muerte la matriz de los ríos.

Oigo pueblos de ayes y valles de lamentos,
veo un bosque de ojos nunca enjutos,
avenidas de lágrimas y mantos:
y en torbenillo de hojas y de vientos,
lutos tras otros lutos y otros lutos,
llantos tras otros llantos y otros llantos.

No aventarán, no arrastrarán tus huesos,
volcán de arrope, trueno de panales,
poeta entretejido, dulce, amargo,
que el calor de los besos
sentiste, entres dos largas hileras de puñales,
largo amor, muerte larga, fuego largo.

Por hacer a tu muerte compañía,
vienen poblando todos los rincones
del cielo y de la tierra bandadas de armonía,

How simple death is: how simple,
but how unjustly snatched away!
It doesn't know to walk slowly, and when
least expected it inflicts its dark wound.

You, the firmest building, destroyed,
you, the highest sparrow hawk, collapsed,
you, the loudest roar,
silent, and more silent, and more silent.

May your happy and illustrious blood fall
like a landslide of ferocious hammers,
over those who arrested you mortally.
May spit and sickles
fall over the stain of their brow.

A poet dies and all creation feels
wounded, twisting its guts.
A cosmic earthquake of cold-sweats
shakes the mountains dreadfully,
a splendor of death moves the wombs of rivers

I hear villages of moans and valleys of lament,
I see a forest of eyes never dry,
avenues of wailing and veils:
and in whirlwinds of leaves and gales,
sorrows atop other sorrows and other sorrows,
weeping atop other weeping and other weeping.

They will not escape, they will not drag your bones,
volcano of thick syrup, thunder of honeycomb,
interwoven poet, sweet, bitter,
you felt the warmth of kisses
between two long rows of daggers,
long love, long death, long fire.

Flocks of harmony,
blue bolts of lightning,
come to keep your death company

relámpagos de azules vibraciones.
Crótalos granizados a montones,
batallones de flautas, panderos y gitanos,
ráfagas de abejorros y violines,
tormentas de guitarras y pianos,
irrupciones de trompas y clarines.

Pero el silencio puede más que tanto instrumento.

Silencioso, desierto, polvoriento
en la muerte desierta,
parece que tu lengua, que tu aliento,
los ha cerrado el golpe de una puerta.

Como si paseara con tu sombra,
paseo con la mía
por una tierra que el silencio alfombra,
que el ciprés apetece más sombría.

Rodea mi garganta tu agonía
como un hierro de horca
y pruebo una bebida funeraria.
Tú sabes, Federico García Lorca,
que soy de los que gozan una muerte diaria.

peopling all the corners of heaven and earth.
Rattlesnakes hailing from the skies,
battalions of flutes, tambourines, and gypsies,
cloudbursts of bumblebees and violins,
storms of guitars and pianos,
irruptions of trumpets and clarions.

But silence is more powerful than any instrument.

Silent, deserted, dust-caked
in the desert of death,
your tongue, your breath,
seem to have thrown the bolt to your door.

As if I walked with your ghost,
I walk with mine
over an earth carpeted in silence,
that the cypress tree would prefer ever darker.

Your agony girdles my throat
like gallows irons
and I taste the funeral potion.
You know, Federico García Lorca,
I am one of those who enjoys a daily death.

TED GENOWAYS

Sentado sobre los muertos
que se han callado en dos meses,
beso zapatos vacíos
y empuño rabiosamente
la mano del corazón
y el alma que lo mantiene.

Que mi voz suba a los montes
y baje a la tierra y truene,
eso pide mi garganta
desde ahora y desde siempre.

Acércate a mi clamor,
pueblo de mi misma leche,
árbolque con tus raíces
encarcelado me tienes,
que aquí estoy yo para amarte
y estoy para defenderte
con la sangre y con la boca
como dos fusiles fieles.

Si yo salí de la tierra,
si yo he nacido de un vientre
desdichado y con pobreza,
no fue sino para hacerme
ruiseñor de las desdichas,
eco de la mala suerte,
y cantar y repetir
a quien escucharme debe
cuanto a penas, cuanto a pobres,
cuanto a tierra se refiere.

Ayer amaneció el pueblo
desnudo y sin qué ponerse,
hambriento y sin qué comer,
y el día de hoy amanece
justamente aborrascado

Sitting upon the dead
fallen silent these two months,
I kiss empty shoes
and make an angry fist
with the heart's hand
and the soul that drives it.

That my voice climb the mountains
and descend to earth as thunder:
this is what my throat begs
now and forever.

Come close to my clamor,
people fed from the same breast,
tree whose roots
keep me in prison,
because I am here to love you
and I am here to defend you
with my blood and with my mouth
like two faithful rifles.

If I came out of the earth,
if I was born from a womb,
pitiful and poor,
it was only that I would become
the nightingale of the pitiful,
echo of bad luck,
to sing and to repeat
to those who must hear me
everything of pain, everything of poverty,
everything of earth.

Yesterday the people woke
stripped and with nothing to cover themselves,
hungry and with nothing to eat,
and now today has dawned
justly hateful

y sangriento justamente.
En su mano los fusiles
leones quieren volverse
para acabar con las fieras
que lo han sido tantas veces.

Aunque te falten las armas
pueblo de cien mil poderes,
no desfallezcan tus huesos,
castiga a quien te malhiere
mientras que te queden puños,
uñas, saliva, y te queden
corazón, entrañas, tripas,
cosas de varón y dientes.
Bravo como el viento bravo,
leve como el aire leve,
asesina al que asesina,
aborrece al que aborrece
la paz de tu corazón
y el vientre de tus mujeres.
No te hieran por la espalda,
vive cara a cara y muere
con el pecho ante las balas,
ancho como las paredes.

Canto con la voz de luto,
pueblo de mí, por tus héroes:
tus ansias como las mías,
tus desventuras que tienen
del mismo metal el llanto,
las penas del mismo temple,
y de la misma madera
tu pensamiento y mi frente,
tu corazón y mi sangre,
tu dolor y mis laureles.
Antemuro de la nada
esta vida me parece.

and justly bloody.
In their hands the rifles
long to become lions
to finish with ferocity those
who have been so many times ferocious.

Even if you have no weapons,
people of one hundred thousand strengths,
don't let your bones thin;
punish those who wound you
as long as you have fists,
fingernails, saliva, and you have
heart, entrails, guts,
testicles and teeth.
Wild as the wild wind,
gentle as the gentle air,
kill those who kill,
hate those who hate
the peace of your heart
and the womb of your women.
Don't let them stab you in the back,
live face to face and die
with your chest before the bullets,
large as a house.

I sing in grief's voice,
my people, for your heroes:
your desires like my own,
your misfortunes that have
the same metal and tears,
your suffering in the same grain
and of the same wood,
your thought and my mind,
your heart and my blood,
your pain and my laurels.
Life looks to me like
a barricade of nothingness.

Aquí estoy para vivir
mientras el alma me suene,
y aquí estoy para morir,
cuando la hora me llegue,
en los veneros del pueblo
desde ahora y desde siempre.
Varios tragos es la vida
y un solo trago es la muerte.

I am here to live
while the soul permits,
and here to die,
when the hour arrives,
in the veins of the people
now and forever.
Life is a lot to swallow,
death is only a gulp.

TED GENOWAYS

Vientos del pueblo me llevan,
vientos del pueblo me arrastran,
me esparcen el corazón
y me avientan la garganta.
Los bueyes doblan la frente,
impotentemente mansa,
delante de los castigos:
los leones la levanta
y al mismo tiempo castigan
con su clamorosa zarpa.
No soy de un pueblo de bueyes
que soy de un pueblo que embargan
yacimiento de leones,
desfiladeros de águilas
y cordillera de toros
con el orgullo en el asta.
Nunca medraron los bueyes
en los páramos de España.
¿Quién habló de echar un yugo
sobre el cuello de esta raza?
¿Quién ha puesto al huracán
jamás ni yugos ni trbas,
ni quién el rayo detuvo
prisionero en un jaula?
Asturianos de braveza,
vascos de piedra blindada,
valencianos de alegría
y castellanos de alma,
labrados como la tierra
y airosos como las alas;
andaluces de relámpago,
nacidos entre guitarras
y forjados en los yunques
torrenciales de las lágrimas;
extremeños de centeno,
gallegos de lluvia y calma,
catalanes de firmeza

Winds of the people carry me,
winds of the people drag me,
scattering my heart
and closing my throat.
Oxen bow their heads,
impotent and meek,
in the face of punishments;
lions raise theirs
and at the same time punish
with their clamorous claw.
I am not from a people of oxen,
I am from a people who seize
the mines of lions,
the mountain passes of eagles
and ridgetops of bulls
with pride in the horn.
Never did oxen prosper
in the wildernesses of Spain.
Who spoke of throwing a yoke
over the neck of this race?
Who ever put yokes
or hobbles on a hurricane,
or kept a lightning bolt
prisoner in a cage?
Asturians of bravery,
Basques of iron-plated stone,
Valencians of mirth
and Castilians of soul,
worked like the soil
and graceful as wings;
Andalusians of lightning flash,
born among guitars
and forged upon torrential
anvils of tears;
Estremadurans of rye,
Galicians of rain and calm,
Catalans of steadiness,

aragoneses de casta,
murcianos de dinamita
frutalmente propagada,
leoneses, navarros, dueños
del hambre, el sudor y el hacha,
reyes de la minería,
señores de la labranza,
hambre que entre las raíces,
como raíces gallardas,
váis de la vida a la muerte,
váis de la nada a la nada:
yugos os quieren poner
gente de la hierba mala,
yugos que habéis de dejar
rotos sobre sus espaldas.
Crepúsculo de los bueyes
está despuntando el alba.
Los bueyes mueren vestidos
de humildad y olor de cuadra:
las águilas, los leones
y los torros, de arrogancia,
y detrás de ellos, el cielo
ni se enturbia ni se acaba.
La agonía de los bueyes
tiene pequeña la cara,
la del animal varón
toda la creación agranda.
Si me muero, que me muera
con la cabeza muy alta.
Muerto y veinte veces muerto,
la boca contra la grama,
tendré apretados los dientes
y decidida la barba.
Cantando espero a la muerte,
que hay ruiseñores que cantan
encima de los fusiles
y en medio de las batallas.

Aragonese of pure line,
Murcians of dynamite
propagated fruitfully,
Leonese, Navarrese, masters
of hunger, sweat, and the ax,
kings of mining,
lords of the tilled soil,
men who, among the roots,
like gallant roots,
go from life to death,
from nothingness to nothingness:
people of the bad seed
want to put yokes on you,
yokes that you must leave
broken across their backs.
Twilight of the oxen
is the dawn breaking.
Oxen die vested in humility
and the stink of stables;
eagles, lions,
and bulls, with pride;
and behind them, the sky
neither darkens nor ends.
The agonized oxen
have a low-spirited gaze,
that of a brute animal,
enlarging all of creation.
If I go out, let me go out
with my head held high.
Dead, twenty times dead,
my mouth against the grama grass,
I'll have my teeth clenched
and my beard determined.
Singing I await death,
for there are nightingales that sing
above the muskets
and in the midst of battles.

TED GENOWAYS

Andaluces de Jaén,
aceituneros altivos,
decidme en el alma: ¿quién,
quién levantó los olivos?

No lo levantó la nada,
ni el dinero, ni el señor,
sino la tierra callada,
el trabajo y el sudor.

Unidos al agua pura
y a los planetas unidos,
los tres dieron la hermosura
de los troncos retorcidos.

Levántate, olivo cano,
dijeron al pie del viento.
Y el olivo alzó una mano
poderosa de cimiento.

Andaluces de Jaén,
aceituneros altivos,
decidme en el alma: ¿quién
amamantó los olivos?

Vuestra sangre, vuestra vida,
no la del explotador
que se enriqueció en la herida
generosa del sudor.

No la del terrateniente
que os sepultó en la pobreza,
que os pisoteó la frente,
que os redujo la cabeza.

Arboles que vuestro afán
consagró al centro del día

Andalusians of Jaén,
proud harvesters of olives,
tell me from your soul: who,
who raised the olive groves?

Not money, not the man;
he did not sweat or toil
to raise them; he did nothing,
on the closed soil.

Together with the pure water
and the aligned planets,
the three gave the beautiful
appearance of twined plants.

Arise, the white olive tree
said to the wind's feet.
And the olive tree raised
a hand solid as concrete.

Andalusians of Jaén,
proud harvesters of olives,
tell me from your soul: who,
who nursed the olive groves?

Your blood, your life,
not those of the culprit
who became rich in the generous
wound of your sweat.

Not that of the landowner
who buried you in poverty,
who beat your brow,
who lowered your eyes.

Trees that your eagerness
consecrated at midday

eran principio de un pan
que sólo el otro comía.

¡Cuántos siglos de aceituna,
los pies y las manos presos,
sol a sol y luna a luna,
pesan sobre vuestros huesos!

Andaluces de Jaén,
aceituneros altivos,
decidme en el alma: ¿ de quién,
de quíen son estos olivos?

Jaén, levántate brava
sobre tus piedras lunares,
no vayas a ser esclava
con todos tus olivares.

Dentro de la claridad
del aceite y sus aromas,
indican tu libertad
la libertad de tus lomas.

were essential to a bread
that only the other ate.

How many centuries of olive,
of imprisoned feet and hands,
sun to sun and moon to moon,
weigh on your bones!

Andalusians of Jaén,
proud harvesters of olives,
ask my soul: who,
who owns the olive groves?

Jaén, arise brave
on your lunar stones,
you are not going to be enslaved
with all your olive groves.

Within the clarity
of the oil and its aromas
appears your liberty,
the liberty of the loam.

TED GENOWAYS

Carne de yugo, ha nacido
más humillado que bello,
con el cuello perseguido
por el yugo para el cuello.

Nace, como la herramientas,
a los golpes destinado,
de una tierra descontenta
y un insatifecho arado.

Entre estiércol puro y vivo
de vacas, trae a la vida
un alma color de olivo
vieja ya y encallecida.

Empieza a vivir, y empieza
a morir de punta a punta
levantando la corteza
de su madre con la yunta.

Empieza a sentir, y siente
la vida como una guerra,
y a dar fatigosamente
en los huesos de la tierra.

Contar sus años no sabe,
y ya sabe que el sudor
es una corona grave
de sal para el labrador.

Trabaja, y mientras trabaja
masculinamente serio,
se unge de lluvia y se alhaja
de carne de cementerio.

A fuerza de golpes, fuerte,
y a fuerza de sol, bruñido,

Flesh for the yoke, he was born
more humble than handsome,
with his neck pursued
by the yoke for his neck.

Born like the tools,
destined for blows
of a discontented land
and an unsatisfied plow.

Amid the pure and strong dung
of cattle, he brings to this life
an olive-colored soul,
old already and callused.

He begins to live and begins
to die from top to bottom
lifting that crust
of his mother with the team.

He begins to feel and feels
this life as if it were a war
and he strikes wearily
against the bones of the earth.

He cannot count his years
and yet he knows that sweat
is a grave crown
of salt for the laborer.

He works and while he works,
masculinely serious,
he is anointed with rain and arrayed
with flesh of the cemetery.

By force of his blows, strong,
and by force of the sun, burnished,

con una ambición de muerte
despedaza un pan reñido.

Cada nuevo día es
más raíz, menos criatura,
que escucha bajo sus pies
la voz de la sepultura.

Y como raíz se hunde
en la tierra lentamente
para que la tierra inunde
de paz y panes su frente.

Me duele este niño hambriento
como una grandiosa espina,
y su vivir ceniciento
resuelve mi alma de encina.

Le veo arar los rastrojos,
y devorar un mendrugo,
y declarar con los ojos
que por qué es carne de yugo.

Me da su arado en el pecho,
y su vida en la garganta,
y sufro viendo el barbecho
tan grande bajo su planta.

¿Quién salvará a este chiquillo
menor que un grano de avena?
¿De dónde saldrá el martillo
verdugo de esta cadena?

Que salga del corazón
de los hombres jornaleros,
que antes de ser hombres son
y han sido niños yunteros.

he tears with death-like ambition
a hard-won loaf of bread.

Each new day he is
more root, less child,
for he hears under his feet
the voice of the grave.

And like the root he sinks
into the ground slowly,
so that the earth is flooded
with peace and his brow with bread.

This hungry child hurts me
like a tremendous thorn
and his ashen life
disturbs my oaken soul.

I see him plow the stubble
and devour a scrap of bread
and declare with his eyes
that his flesh is for the yoke.

His plow strikes me in the heart
and his life in my throat,
and I suffer seeing the fallow
so large beneath his sole.

Who will save this little boy,
smaller than a grain of oats?
Where will the hammer come from,
that executioner of this chain?

Let it come from the heart
of these day-laboring men,
who before becoming men are
and have been plowboys.

TED GENOWAYS

I.

Naciones de la tierra, patrias del mar, hermanos
del mundo y de la nada:
habitantes perdidos y lejanos,
más que del corazón, de la mirada.

Aquí tengo una voz enardecida,
aquí tengo una vida combatida y airada,
aquí tengo un rumor , aquí tengo una vida.

Abierto estoy, mirad, como una herida.
Hundido estoy, mirad, estoy hundido
en medio de mi pueblo y de sus males.
Herido voy, herido y malherido,
sangrando por trincheras y hospitales.

Hombres , mundos, naciones,
atended, escuchad mi sangrante sonido,
recoged mis latidos de quebranto
en vuestros espaciosos corazones,
porque yo empuño el alma cuando canto.

Cantando me defiendo
y defiendo mi pueblo cuando en mi pueblo imprimen
su herradura de pólvora y estruendo
los bárbaros del crimen.

Esta es su obra, esta:
pasan , arrasan como torbellinos,
y son ante su cólera funesta
armas los horizontes y muertes los caminos.

El llanto que por valles y balcones se vierte,
en las piedras diluvia y en piedras trabaja,
y no hay espacio para tanta muerte,
y no hay madera para tanta caja.

I.

Nations of the earth, fatherlands of the sea, brothers
of the world and of nothingness:
inhabitants, lost and farther
from sight than the heart.

Here I have a voice impassioned,
here I have a life embattled and angered,
here I have a rumor, but here I have a life.

I am open, look, like a wound.
I am drowned, look, drowned
in the midst of my people and their ills.
I go wounded, wounded and maimed,
bleeding through trenches and hospitals.

Men, worlds, nations,
pay heed, listen to my bleeding cry,
gather my breaking heartbeats
into your spacious hearts,
because I clutch the soul when I sing.

Singing I defend myself
and I defend my people when the barbarians
of this crime would stamp them
with their hooves of gunpowder and clamor.

This is their work, this:
passing, razing like whirlwinds,
and before their dismal bile
the horizons are arms and the roads are death.

The lament pouring through valley and balconies,
deluges the stones and works in the stones,
and there is no room for so much death
and there is no wood for so many coffins.

Caravanas de cuerpos abatidos.
Todos vendajes, penas y pañuelos:
todo camillas donde a los heridos
se les quiebran las fuerzas y los vuelos.
Sangre, sangre por árboles y suelos,
sangre por aguas, sangre por paredes,
y un temor de que España se desplome
del peso de la sangre que moja entre sus redes
hasta el pan que se come.

Recoged este viento,
naciones, hombres, mundos
que parte de las bocas de conmovido aliento
y de los hospitales moribundos.

Aplicad las orejas
a mi clamor de pueblo atropellado,
al ¡ay! de tantas madres, a las quejas
de tanto ser luciente que el luto ha devorado.

Los pechos que empujaban y herían las montañas,
vedlos desfallecidos sin leche ni hermosura,
y ved las blancas novias y las negras pestañas
caídas y sumidas en una siesta oscura.

Aplicad la pasión de las entrañas
a este pueblo que muere con un gesto invencible
sembrados por los labios y la frente,
bajo los implacables aeroplanos
que arrebatan terrible,
terrible, ignominiosa, diariamente,
a las madres los hijos de las manos.

Ciudades de trabajo y de inocencia,
juventudes que brotan de la encina,
troncos de bronce, cuerpos de potencia
yacen precipitados en la ruina.

Caravans of beaten-down bodies.
All is bandages, pain, and handkerchiefs,
all is stretchers on which the wounded
have broken their strength and their wings.
Blood, blood through the trees and the soil,
blood in the waters and on the walls,
and a fear that Spain will collapse
from the weight of the blood which soaks through her
    meshes
right to the bread which is eaten.

Gather together this gale,
nations, men, worlds,
which proceeds from the mouths of the impassioned breath
and from hospitals of the dying.

Apply your ears
to my clamor of a violated people,
to the *oh!* of so many mothers, to the groans
of many a lucid being whom grief devoured.

The breasts which drove and wounded the mountains
see them languish without milk or beauty,
and see the white sweethearts and the black eyelashes
fallen and submissive in an obscure siesta.

Apply the passion of your entrails
to this people which dies with an invincible gesture
scattered by the lips and the brow,
beneath the implacable airplanes
which snatch terribly,
terribly ignominiously, every day,
sons from the hands of their mothers.

Cities of the world and innocence,
youths who blossom from the oak,
trunks of bronze, bodies of potency,
lie fallen into ruin.

Un porvenir de polvo se avecina,
se avecina un suceso
en que no quedará ninguna cosa:
ni piedra sobre piedra ni hueso sobre hueso.

España no es España, que es una inmensa fosa,
que es un gran cementerio rojo y bombardeado:
los bárbaros la quieren de este modo.

Será la tierra un denso corazón desolado,
si vosotros, naciones, hombres, mundos,
con mi pueblo del todo
y vuestro pueblo encima del costado,
no quebráis los colmillos iracundos.

II.

Pero no lo será: que un mar pifiante,
triunfante siempre, siempre decidido,
hecho por la luz, para la hazaña,
agita su cabeza de rebelde diamante,
bate su pie calzado en el sonido
por todos los cadáveres de España.

Es una juventud: recoged este viento.
Su sangre es el cristal que no se empaña,
su sombrero el laurel y el pedernal su aliento.

Donde clava la fuerza de sus dientes
brota un volcán de diáfanas espadas,
y sus hombros batientes,
y sus talones guían llamaradas.

Esta compuesta de hombres del trabajo
de herreros rojos, de albos albañiles,
de yunteros con rostro de cosechas.

A future of dust advances,
a fate advances
in which nothing will remain:
not stone on stone nor bone on bone.

Spain is not Spain, it is an immense trench,
a vast cemetery red and bombarded:
the barbarians have willed it so.

The earth will be a dense heart, desolated,
if you, nations, men, worlds,
with the whole of my people,
and yours as well on your side,
do not break the ferocious fangs.

II.

But that won't be: for a stomping sea,
triumphant always, always resolute,
made for the light, for heroic exploit,
shakes its head of rebellious diamond,
pounds its shod foot on the sound
for all the cadavers of Spain.

It's a generation of youth: gather this wind.
Their blood is the glass that never fogs;
their hat, the laurel; and the flint, their life's breath.

Wherever they clench their teeth,
a volcano of transparent swords erupts,
their shoulders swinging,
their heels shooting flames.

It's composed of men who work:
of red blacksmiths, white stonemasons,
plowmen with harvest faces.

Oceánicamente transcurren por debajo
de un fragor de sirenas y herramientas fabriles
y de gigantes arcos alumbrados con flechas.

A pesar de la muerte, estos varones
con metal y relámpagos igual que los escudos,
hacen retroceder a los cañones
acobardados, temblorosos, mudos.

El polvo no los puede y hacen del polvo fuego,
savia, explosión, verdura repentina:
con su poder de abril apasionado
precipitan el alma del espliego,
el parto de la mina,
el fértil movimiento del arado.

Ellos harán de cada ruina un prado,
de cada pena un fruto de alegría,
de España un firmamento de hermosura.
Vedlos agigantar el mediodía,
y hermosearlo todo con su joven bravura.

Se merecen la espuma de los truenos,
se merecen la vida y el olor del olivo,
los españoles amplios y serenos
que mueven la mirada como un pájaro altivo.

Naciones, hombres, mundos, esto escribo:
la juventud de España saldrá de las trincheras
de pie, invencible como la semilla,
pues tiene un alma llena de banderas
que jamás se asomete ni arrodilla.

Allí van por los yermos de Castilla
los cuerpos que parecen potros batalladores,
toros de victorioso desenlace,
diciéndose en su sangre de generosas flores
que morir es la cosa mas grande que se hace.

Sea-like they pass time beneath
a din of sirens and manufacturing tools
and gigantic arcs illuminated by arrows.

Despite death, these good men,
with metal and lightning like shields,
make the cannons retreat
intimidated, trembling, silenced.

Gunpowder was powerless against them, they made fire
    from it,
sap, explosion, sudden greens:
with the power of their impassioned flower of youth
they quickened the soul of the lavender,
the product of the mine,
the fertile movement of the plough.

They will make a meadow from each ruin;
out of each sorrow, a fruit of happiness;
out of Spain, a firmament of beauty.
Look at them making the midday gigantic
and beautiful with their youthful bravery.

They deserve the foam of thunderclaps,
they deserve life and the scent of the olive tree,
these ample and serene Spaniards
who glance about like a proud bird.

Nations, men, world, this I write:
the youth of Spain will leave the trenches
on foot, invincible like the seed,
for they have a soul filled with banners
that never submits nor falls to its knees.

There over the barren plains of Castile travel
these bodies that seem to be battling colts,
bulls of victorious outcome,
expressing with their blood of generous flowers
that dying is the greatest thing one can do.

Quedaran en el tiempo vencedores,
siempre de sol y majestad cubiertos,
los guerreros de huesos tan gallardos
que si son muertos son gallardos muertos:
la juventud que a España salvara aunque tuviera
que combatir con un fusil de nardos
y una espada de cera.

In time they will be left the victors,
forever covered in sun and majesty,
these warriors of such gallant bones,
for if they're dead men, they're gallant dead men:
these youths will save Spain, even if they have
to fight with rifles of jasmine
and a shotgun of wax.

TED GENOWAYS

Si hay hombres que contienen un alma sin fronteras,
una esparcida frente de mundiales cabellos,
cubierta de horizontes, barcos y cordilleras,
con arena y con nieve, tú eres uno de aquellos.

Las patrias te llamaron con todas sus banderas,
que tu aliento llenara de movimientos bellos.
Quisiste apaciguar la sed de las panteras,
y flamaste enchido contra sus atropellos.

Con un sabor a todos los soles y los mares,
España te recoge porque en ella realices
tu majestad de árbol que abarca un continente.

A través de tus huesos irán los olivares
desplegando en tierra sus más férreas raíces,
abrazando a los hombres universal, fielmente.

If there are men who contain a soul without frontiers,
a brow scattered with universal hair,
covered with horizons, ships, and mountain chains,
with sand and with snow, then you are one of those.

Fatherlands called to you with all their banners,
so that your breath filled with beautiful movements.
You wanted to quench the thirst of panthers
and fluttered full against their abuses.

With a taste of all suns and seas,
Spain beckons you because in her you realize
your majesty like a tree that embraces a continent.

Around your bones, the olive groves will grow,
unfolding their iron roots in the ground,
embracing men universally, faithfully.

TED GENOWAYS

En el mar halla el agua su paraíso ansiado
y el sudor su horizonte, su fragor, su plumaje.
El sudor es un árbol desbordante y salado,
un voraz oleaje.

Llega desde la edad del mundo más remota
a ofrecer a la tierra su copa sacudida,
a sustentar la sed y la sal gota a gota,
a iluminar la vida.

Hijo del movimiento, primo del sol, hermano
de la lágrima, deja rodando por las eras,
del abril al octubre, del invierno al verano,
áureas enredaderas.

Cuando los campesinos van por la madrugada
a favor de la esteva removiendo el reposo,
se visten una blusa silenciosa y dorada
de sudor silencioso.

Vestidura de oro de los trabajadores,
adorno de las manos como de las pupilas.
Por la atmósfera esparce sus fecundos olores
una lluvia de axilas.

El sabor de la tierra se enriquece y madura:
caen los copos del llanto laborioso y oliente,
maná de los varones y de la agricultura,
bebida de mi frente.

Los que no habéis sudado jamás, los que andáis yertos
en el ocio sin brazos, sin música, sin poros,
no usaréis la corona de los poros abiertos
ni el poder de los toros.

Viviréis maloliendo, moriréis apagados:
la encendida hermosura reside en los talones

Water drinks its paradise in the sea,
and sweat finds horizon, uproar, crest.
Sweat is a brimming salty tree,
a greedy surf.

To offer the land its trembling cup
sweat reaches from earth's farthest age,
feeds thirst and salt drop by drop,
to kindle life.

Sun's cousin, tear's brother, motion's child,
April to October, winter to summer.
it goes rolling through the field
in golden vines.

As peasants pass through dawn
behind the plough that uproots their sleep,
they each wear a silent workshirt brown
with mute sweat.

The worker's golden robe,
jewel of the hands and eyes as well,
through the haze the axilla's shower
spreads a fecund smell.

The land's flavor grows ripe and rich:
flakes that hardworking, pungent weeping yields,
manna of the men and fields,
my forehead's drink.

You who never feel stiff or sweat,
at leisure with no arms, music, pores,
will never feel the open pores' wet
halo, or the power of the bulls.

You will live stinking, die snuffed out:
fiery beauty takes up life in the heels

de los cuerpos que mueven sus miembros trabajados
como constelaciones.

Entregad al trabajo, compañeros, las frentes:
que el sudor, con su espada de sabrosos cristales,
con sus lentos diluvios, os hará transparentes,
venturosos, iguales.

of bodies whose working limbs shift about
like constellations.

Comrades, surrender your foreheads to work:
sweat, with its sword of tasty crystal,
with its sticky flood, makes you transparent,
lucky, equal.

DON SHARE

He poblado tu vientre de amor y sementera
he prolongado el eco de sangre a que respondo
y espero sobre el surco como el arado espera:
he llegado hasta el fondo.

Morena de altas torrres, alta luz y ojos altos,
esposa de piel, gran trago de mi vida,
tus pechos locos crecen hacia mi dando saltos
de cierva concebida.

Ya me parece que eres un cristal delicado,
temo que te me rompas al mas leve tropiezo
y a reforzar tus penas con mi piel de soldado
fuera como el cerezo.

Espejo de mi carne, sustento de mis alas,
te doy vida en la muerte que me dan y no tomo.
Mujer, mujer te quiero cercado por las balas,
ansiado por el plomo.

Sobre los ataúdes feroces en acecho,
sobre los mismos muertos sin remedio y sin fosa
te quiero, y te quisiera besar con todo el pecho
hasta en el polvo, esposa.

Cuando junto a los campos de combate te piensa
mi frente que no enfría ni aplaca tu figura,
te acercas hacia mí como una loca inmensa
de hambrienta dentadura.

Escríbeme a la lucha, siénteme en la trinchera:
aquí con el fusil tu nombre evoco y fijo,
y defiendo tu vientre de pobre que me espera,
y defiendo tu hijo.

Nacerá nuestro hijo con el puño cerrado,
envuelto en un clamor de victoria y guitarras,

I have sown your womb with love and seed,
have prolonged the echo of blood which I answer
and I wait in the furrow the way the plow waits:
I've touched the depths.

Dark-skinned woman of tall towers, tall lights, and tall eyes,
wife of my skin, deep gulp of my life,
your crazy breasts swell toward me, bounding
like a pregnant doe.

It seems to me that you are a delicate crystal,
I fear the lightest touch will break you,
and I come to reinforce your veins with my soldier's skin
like a cherry tree.

Mirror of my flesh, support of my wings,
I give you life in the death they give me but will not take.
Woman, woman, I love you, surrounded by bullets,
worried by lead.

Over the fierce coffins in ambush,
over the same dead without remedy or grave,
I love you, and I want to kiss you with all my heart,
until we turn to dust, my wife.

When I near the battlefields, I think of you,
my brow neither cooling nor quieting your image,
you surround me like an immense mouth
of hungry teeth.

Write to me at war, feel for me in the trench:
here I invoke your name, fix it with my rifle,
and defend your peasant womb awaiting me,
and defend your child.

Our child will be born with a closed fist,
wrapped in the clamor of victory and guitars,

y dejaré a tu puerta mi vida de soldado
sin colmillos ni garra.

Es preciso matar para seguir viviendo.
Un dia iré a la sombra de tu pelo lejano,
y dormiré en la sábana de almidón y de estruendo
cosida por tu mano.

Tus piernas implacables al parto van derechas,
y tu implacable boca de labios indomables,
y ante mi soledad de explosiones y de brechas
recorres un camino de besos implacables.

Para el hijo será la paz que estoy forjando.
Y al fin en océano de irremediables huesos
tu corazón y el mío naufragarán, quedando
una mujer y un hombre gastados por los besos.

and I will leave my soldier's life at your door
without fangs or claws.

To go on living, one must kill.
One day I will enter into the shadows of your distant hair,
and I will sleep in sheets, starched and thundering,
sewn by your hand.

Your implacable legs parted straight forward,
and your implacable mouth with its indomitable lips,
and where before my solitude was breached by
    explosions,
you mend the roads with your implacable kisses.

I am forging peace for the child.
And in the end in an ocean of incurable bones
your heart and mine will shipwreck, stranding
a woman and a man worn out by kisses.

TED GENOWAYS

[POEMAS SUELTOS]
(1937)

[UNCOLLECTED POEMS]
(1937)

Hombres que nunca veía,
porque no tengo bastantes
ojos para tanto ver,
cuerpo para tantas partes:
hombres que lejos de mí,
aunque hasta mí se acercasen,
vivían como eclipsados
bajo el eclipse del traje,
de repentre se aproximan
a mis ojos, a mi carne,
a mi corazón poblado
de batallas y habitantes.
Se aproximan, se desnudan,
se desoscurecen y arden,
y para siempre en mi frente
graban la luz de su imagen.

Ayer te desconocía
en medio de los eriales,
de paso por las encinas,
en el resplandor del aire
y en el resplandor rabioso
de las bombas y los tanques.
Ayer no hacía memoria
de ti, teniente González.
Hoy te conozco y publico
tus ímpetus de oleaje,
tu sencillez de eucaplipto,
tu corazón de combate,
digno de ser capitán,
digno de ser comandante.

Aquel día del enero
salió prometiendo sangre
al cielo de la mañana
y a la tierra de la tarde.

Men whom I have never seen,
because I don't have enough
eyes to see so much,
a body of so many parts:
men far away from me,
although they approach me,
they lived like the hidden
under the eclipse of a uniform,
all of a sudden they draw close
to my eyes, to my flesh,
to my heart filled
with battles and people.
They draw near, casting off their clothes,
brightening and bursting into flame,
and forever in my mind
they engrave the light of their image.

Yesterday I did not know you
in the middle of the fallow fields,
on the way through the green oaks,
in the splendor of the air
and in the rabid splendor
of bombs and tanks.
Yesterday I had no memory
of you, Lieutenant González.
Today I know you and proclaim
your surging impulses,
your simplicity of eucalyptus,
your heart of combat,
worthy of being a captain,
worthy of being a commander.

That day in January
left promising blood
to the sky of the morning
and to the earth of the afternoon.

El alba pasó ante un grupo
foragido de alemanes,
carnívoro de italianos,
cagado de generales,
y el sol apuntó queriendo
inundarlos de vinagre.
La luz se halló entre cañones,
rocío entre cadáveres,
el azul y sus laureles
y el valor entre encinares,
sobre las frentes erguidas,
sobre los huesos tajantes,
sobre la piel de una tropa
de campesinos leales.

Se oyó una voz torrencial,
se alzó un brazo detonante:
eran los de Valentín,
que como tres huracanes
campaba cuando decía:
¡Que no retroceda nadie!
¡Que la muerte nos encuentre
yendo siempre hacia adelante
o dentro de las trincheras
firmes lo mismo que árboles;
a cada herida más fieros,
más duros a cada ataque,
más grandes a cada asalto
y a cada muerte más grandes!
¡Y al que ofrezca las espaldas
al enemigo, matadle!

La guerra se hermoseaba
al pie de sus ademanes.
Tronaron las baterías
nutridas de tempestades,
y la voz del Campesino
no cesaba de escucharse

The dawn passed before a group of
German outlaws,
carnivorous Italians,
shit-stacked generals,
and the sun aimed wanting
to flood them with vinegar.
Daybreak found itself among cannons,
dew among corpses,
the blue and its laurels
and valor found itself in the oak groves,
on the pride-swollen brows,
on the cutting bones,
on the skin of a troop
of loyal campesinos.

A torrential voice was heard,
a detonating arm was raised:
they were those of Valentín,
which, like three hurricanes,
would halt when he said:
No one retreat!
May death find us
always pushing forward
or in the trenches
firm as trees;
fiercer with each wound,
harder with each attack,
grander with each assault,
and greater with each death!
And any who offers his back
to the enemy, kill him!

The war grew beautiful
at the foot of his stance.
The batteries thundered
fed by storms,
and the voice of the campesino
did not cease to be heard

ni de iluminar el humo
de la pólvora salvaje.

El teniente de Leal,
González el admirable,
no apartaba de la oreja
aquella voz desbordante,
y echó en su puesto raíces
de heroísmo y de romance.

Por tres veces con tres plomos,
vino la muerte a buscarle:
tres heridas le clavaron
tres fusiles criminales,
y a pesar del enemigo,
y a pesar de los pesares,
su juventud parecía
una cumbre invulernable,
una bandera invencible
y campeadora y gigante.

Cuando perdieron tus venas
fuerzas con qué sustenarse
y la sangre te sonaba
por los bolsillos, González,
no pediste un hospital
como piden los cobardes,
que pediste una camilla
sobre la que reclinarte
para seguir disparando,
mandando fuego y coraje.

¡Mirad qué ademán tan alto,
mirad qué pecho tan fácil
al viento varón y extenso
de las generosidades!
Mujeres que vais al fondo
de la vida a haceros madres:
vuestros abrazos fecundos,

nor to illuminate the smoke
of the savage gunpowder.

The Loyalist lieutenant,
González the admirable,
did not turn his ear
from that flooding voice
and put down roots
of heroism and of romance.

Three times with three bullets,
death came to find him:
three wounds nailed him,
three criminal barrels,
and in spite of the enemy,
and in spite of the sorrows,
his youth appeared
an invulnerable summit,
an invincible, gigantic
outstandingly brave banner.

When your veins lost their power
to sustain themselves
and the blood that spoke to you
through your pockets, González,
you did not beg for a hospital
like the begging cowards,
you did beg for a stretcher
over which to recline
in order to continue to shoot,
delivering courage and fire.

Look at the posture so tall,
look at the chest so easy
to break open to the wind
and so extensively generous!
Women who come to the well
of life to become mothers:
your fertile embraces,

vuestros vientres palpitantes,
hombre de tanto tamaño
sólo merecen poblarles.
Llevan el pueblo en los huesos
y el mediodía en la sangre.

your palpitating wombs,
only men of such stature
deserve to populate you.
They carry the people in their bones
and the midday sun in their blood.

TED GENOWAYS

El alba del diecenueve
de julio no se atrevía
a precipitar el día
sobre su costa de nieve.
Nadie a despertar se atreve
hosco de presentimiento.
Y el viento del pueblo, el viento
que muevo y aliento yo
pasó a mi lado y pasó
hacia el 5º Regimiento.

Me desperté entre cañones,
y pistolas y aeroplanos,
y un río de milicianos
como un río de leones.
Eran varios corazones
los que en el pecho sentía:
la sublevación ardía,
disparaba, aullaba en torno,
y era el corazón de un horno
el gran corazón del día.

Hombres de noble mirada
y de condición más noble,
que han hecho temblar al roble
y desmayarse a la espalda:
héroes que parió la nada,
dejando sin movimiento
el monte, el campo, el aliento
de la paz y la labor,
iban a unir su valor
en el 5º Regimiento.

Herrerías y poblados,
minas, talleres y eras
ante las cajas guerreras
enmudecieron parados.

The dawn of the 29th
of July did not dare
to hurry the day
over its snow-white shore.
Sullen with misgiving
no one dared to awake.
And the wind of the people, the wind
that moved and inspired me
passed by my side and
toward the 5th Regiment.

I woke amid cannons,
and pistols and airplanes,
and a river of militiamen
like a river of lions.
It felt in my chest as if
there were many hearts:
an insurrection burned,
shooting, howling around me,
it was the core of a furnace
the great heart of the day.

Men of noble appearance
and of the highest rank,
who have made the oak tree tremble
and swoon in the face of the sword:
heroes born from nothingness,
leaving without movement
the mountain, the field, the spirit
of peace and labor,
going to gather their valor
in the 5th Regiment.

Forges and villages,
mines, workshops, and threshing floors
before war coffins
were left standing mute.

Se marchaban los arados,
y las demás herramientas,
a las casas cenicientas
donde la pobreza anida
al aparecer la vida
con pólvoras y tormentas.

Campesinos: segadores,
la fama de los yunteros,
la historia de los herreros
y la flor de los sudores:
albañiles y pastores,
Los hombres de sufrimiento,
ante el fatal movimiento
que atropellarlos quería,
fueron a dar su energía
en el 5º Regimiento.

Lejos de los minerales,
los mineros más profundos
se movían iracundos
como los fieros metals;
ausentes de los trigales
y de los besos ausentes,
los campesinos vehementes,
con una sonrisa hostil,
iban detrás del fusil
y de las malvadas gentes.

¡Que largamente seguros
lucharon bajo sus ceños,
qué oscuramente risueños
y qué claramente oscuros!
Eran como errantes muros
generosos de cimiento,
y si llegaba el momento
de morir daban su vida
como una luz encendida
par el 5º Regimiento.

The ploughs and other
tools marched away
to the ashen houses
where poverty dwells,
at the arrival of life
with gunpowder and storms.

Campesinos: harvesters,
fame of ox-tamers,
fable of blacksmiths
and the fruit of their sweat:
masons and shepherds.
Men of suffering,
before the fatal movement
that wanted to trample them,
went on to give their energy
to the 5th Regiment.

Far from the mine-shafts,
those deepest miners
moved feverishly
like metal fires;
absent from the wheatfields
and absent from kisses,
the vehement campesinos,
with a hostile smile,
went after the rifles
and after the wicked people.

How strongly gunlocks
fought under their frowns,
how obscurely smiling
and how clearly obscure!
They were like errant walls
hardened with cement,
and if the moment of death
arrived, they gave their lives
like a burning light
for the 5th Regiment.

¡Cuantos quedaron allí
donde cuántos no quedaron
y cuántos se recostaron
donde cuántos de pie vi!
Así cayeron, así:
como gigantes lucientes,
enarboladas las frentes
con un orgullo de lanza,
y una expresión de venganza
alrededor de los dientes.

España será de España
y español el español
que lleva en la sangre un sol
y en cada gota una hazaña.
No seremos de Alemania
en ningún negro momento
porque el puro sentimiento
que nutre a los españoles
seguirá dando sus soles
para el 5º Regimiento.

How many remained there
where so many did not remain
and where so many were lying down
where I saw so many walking!
Thus they fell, thus:
like luminous giants,
heads held high
with pride of a pikeman,
an expression of vengeance
clenched in their teeth.

Spain will belong to Spain
and a Spaniard will be the Spaniard
that carries a sun in the blood
and in each drop a heroic feat.
We will not belong to Germany
in any black moment
because the pure feeling
that feeds the Spaniards
will continue bringing the sun
for the 5th Regiment.

TED GENOWAYS

Que vienen, vienen, vienen
los lentos, lentos, lentos,
los ávidos, los fúnebres,
los aéreos carniceros.

Que nunca, nunca, nunca
su tenebroso vuelo
podrá ser confundido
con el de los jilgueros.

Que asaltan las palomas
sin hiel. Que van sedientos
de sangre, sangre, sangre,
de cuerpos, cuerpos, cuerpos.

Que el mundo no es el mundo.
Que el cielo no es el cielo,
sino el rincón del crimen
más negro, negro, negro.

Que han deshonrado al pájaro.
Que van de pueblo en pueblo,
desolación y ruina
sembrando, removiendo.

Que vienen, vienen, vienen
con sed de cementerio
dejando atrás un rastro
de muertos, muertos, muertos.

Que ven los hospitales
lo mismo que los cuervos.

Que nadie duerme, nadie.
Que nadie está despierto.
Que toda madre vive
pendiente del silencio,

How they come, they come, they come,
those sluggards, sluggards, sluggards,
those gluttons, those funerals,
those butcherous airplanes.

How their dark flight
will never, never, never
be confounded
by the flight of linnets.

How they assault doves
without bitterness. How they thirst
for blood, blood, blood,
for bodies, bodies, bodies.

How the world is not the world.
How the sky is not the sky,
rather the corner of crime
darkening, darkening, darkening.

How they have dishonored the bird.
How they lay ruin and desolation
to village after village,
scattering and stirring.

How they come, they come, they come
with thirst for the cemetery
leaving behind a trail
of the dead, the dead, the dead.

How they look at the hospitals
the same as crows.

How nobody sleeps, nobody.
How nobody is awake.
How every mother
hangs on the silence,

del ay de la sirena,
con la ansiedad al cuello,
sin voz, sin paz, sin casa,
sin sueño.

Que nadie, nadie, nadie
lo olvide ni un momento.
Que no es posible el crimen.
Que no es posible esto.
Que tierra nuestra quieren.
Que tierra les daremos
en un hoyo, a puñados:
que queden satisfechos.

Que caigan, caigan: caigan.
Que fuego, fuego: fuego.

on the wailing siren
with anguish in her throat,
without voice, without peace, without home,
without sleep.

How nobody, nobody, nobody
could forget even a moment.
How this crime is not possible.
How this is not possible.
How they want our land.
How we will toss it
into a pit, by handfuls:
until they are satisfied.

May they fall, fall: fall.
What fire, fire: fire.

TED GENOWAYS

[LETRILLA DE UNA CANCIÓN DE GUERRA]

Déjame que me vaya,
Madre, a la guerra.
Déjame, blanca hermana,
Novia morena.
Déjame.

Y depués de dejarme
Junto a las balas,
Mándame a la trinchera
Besos y cartas.
Mandame.

[WAR LYRIC]

Let me go,
mother, to the war.
Let me, fair sister,
dark-skinned bride.
Let me.

And after you have let me
close to the bullets,
send me in the trenches
kisses and letters.
Send me.

TED GENOWAYS

[EL HOMBRE ACECHA]
(1939)

[MAN IS A HUNTER]
(1939)

Pablo: Te oigo, te recuerdo en esa tierra tuya, luchando con tu voz frente a los aluviones que arrebatan la vaca y la niña para proyectarlas en tu pecho. Oigo tus pasos hechos a cruzar la noche, que vuelven a sonar sobre las losas de Madrid, junto a Federico, a Vicente, a Delia, a mí mismo. Y recuerdo a nuestro alrededor aquellas madrugadas, cuando amanecíamos dentro del azul de un topacio de carne universal; en el umbral de la taberna confuso de llanto y escarcha, como viudos y heridos de la luna.

Pablo: Un rosal sombrío viene y se cierne sobre mí, sobre una cuna familiar que se desfonda poco a poco, hasta entreverse dentro de ella, además de un niño de sufrimiento, el fondo de la tierra. Ahora recuerdo y comprendo más tu combatida casa, y me pregunto: ¿qué tenía que ver con el consulado cuando era cónsul Pablo?

Tú preguntas por el corazón, y yo también. Mira cuántas bocas cenicientas de rencor, hambre, muerte, pálidas de no cantar, no reír: resecas de no entregarse al beso profundo. Pero mira el pueblo que sonríe con una florida tristeza, augurando el porvenir de la alegre substancia. El nos resonderá. Y las tabernas, hoy tenebrosas como funerarias, irradiarán el resplandor más penetrante del vino y la poesía.

Pablo: I hear you, I remember you on that land of yours, fighting with your voice in front of the floods that snatch the cow and the girl to display them on your chest. I hear your footsteps meant to cross the night, that echo again over the slabs of Madrid, together with Federico, with Vicente, with Delia, and with me alike. And I remember those dawns around us, when dawn would catch us in the topaz blue of universal flesh; in the threshold of the tavern confused by tears and frost, like widowers and wounded by the moon.

Pablo: A somber rosebush comes and blooms over me, over a familiar cradle that sinks little by little, until I glimpse within it, besides a boy of suffering, the bottom of the earth. Now I remember and understand better your embattled house, and I ask myself: what did it have to do with the consulate when Pablo was consul?

You ask for the heart, and I do too. Look how many mouths ashen with resentment, hunger, death, pale from not singing, not laughing: parched from not giving themselves to a profound kiss. But look how the people smile with a flowery sadness, auguring the substance of happiness to come. It will respond to us. And the taverns, today gloomy as funeral parlors, will radiate the most penetrating brilliance of wine and poetry.

TED GENOWAYS

Se ha retirado el campo
al ver abalanzarse
crispadamente al hombre.

¡Qué abismo entre el olivo
y el hombre se descubre!

El animal que canta:
el animal que puede
llorar y echar raíces,
rememoró sus garras.

Garras que revestía
de suavidad y flores,
pero que, al fin, desnuda
en toda su crueldad.

Crepitan en mis manos.
Aparta de ellas, hijo.
Estoy dispuesto a hundirlas,
dispuesto a proyectarlas,
sobre tu carne leve.

He régresado al tigre.
Aparta o te destrozo.

Hoy el amor es muerte,
y el hombre acecha al hombre.

The field has drawn back
when it saw man, muscles
tightened, rush into it.

What an abyss appears
between the olive tree and man!

The animal who sings:
the animal who is able
to weep and to sink roots,
remembered his claws.

Claws that he adorned
with silkiness and flowers
but at last allows to be bare
in all their cruelty.

My claws are snapping on my hands.
Keep away from them, my son.
I am liable to plunge them,
I am liable to thrust them
into your fragile body.

I have turned back into the tiger.
Keep away, or I will destroy you.

Today love is death,
and man is a hunter of man.

JAMES WRIGHT

Diciembre ha congelado su aliento de dos filos,
y lo resopla desde los cielos congelados,
como una llama seca desarrollada en hilos,
como una larga ruina que atraca a los soldados.

Nieve donde el caballo que impone sus pisadas
es una soledad de galopante luto.
Nieve de uñas cernidas, de garras derribadas,
de celeste maldad, de desprecio absoluto.

Muerde, tala, traspasa como un tremendo hachazo,
con un hacha de mármol encarnizado y leve.
Desciende, se derrama con un deshecho abrazo
de precipicios y alas, de soledad y nieve.

Esta agresión que parte del centro del invierno,
hambre cruda, cansada de tener hambre y frío,
amenaza al desnudo con un rencor eterno,
blanco, mortal, hambriento, silencioso, sombrío.

Quiere aplacar las fraguas, los odios, las hogueras,
quiere cegar los mares, sepultar los amores:
y va elevando lentas y diáfanas barreras,
estatuas silenciosas y vidrios agresores.

Que se derrarne a chorros el corazón de lana
de tantos almacenes y talleres textiles,
para cubrir los cuerpos que queman la mañana
con la voz, la mirada, los pies y los fusiles.

Ropa para los cuerpos que pueden ir desnudos,
que pueden ir vestidos de escarchas y de hielos:
de piedra enjuta contra los picotazos rudos,
las mordeduras pálidas y los pálidos vuelos.

Ropa para los cuerpos que rechazan callados
los ataques más blancos con los huesos más rojos.

December has frozen its double-edged breath
and blows it down from the icy heavens,
like a dry fire coming apart in threads,
like a huge ruin that topples on soldiers.

Snow where horses have left their hoof-marks
is a solitude of grief that gallops on.
Snow like split fingernails, or claws badly worn,
like a malice out of heaven or a final contempt.

It bites, prunes, cuts through with the heavy
slash of a bloodshot and pale marble ax.
It comes down, it falls everywhere like some ruined
    embrace
of canyons and wings, solitude and snow.

This violence that splits off from the core of winter,
raw hunger tired of being hungry and cold,
hangs over the naked with an eternal grudge
that is white, speechless, dark, starving, and fatal.

It wants to soften down forges, hatred, flames,
it wants to stop up the seas, to bury all loves.
It goes along throwing up huge, gauzy drifts,
hostile hunks of glass, statues that say nothing.

I want the heart made of wood in every shop
and textile factory to flood over and cover
the bodies that ignite the morning
with their looks and yells, boots and rifles.

Clothes for the corpses that are able to go naked,
able to go dressed in frost and ice,
in withered stone that fights off the cruel beaks,
the pale beak thrusts and the pale escapes.

Clothes for corpses that silently fall back
the most snowy attacks with the reddest bones.

Porque tienen el hueso solar estos soldados,
y porque son hogueras con pisadas, con ojos.

La frialdad se abalanza, la muerte se deshoja,
el clamor que no suena, pero que escucho, llueve.
Sobre la nieve blanca, la vida roja y roja
hace la nieve cálida, siembra fuego en la nieve.

Tan decididamente son el cristal de roca
que sólo el fuego, sólo la llama cristaliza,
que atacan con el pómulo nevado, con la boca,
y vuelven cuanto atacan recuerdos de ceniza.

Because these soldiers have sun-fired bones,
because they are fires with footprints and eyes.

The cold hunches forward, death loses its leaves.
I can hear the noiseless sound raining down.
Red on the white snow, life turns
the steamy snow red, sows fire in the snow.

Soldiers are so much like rock crystals
that only fire, only flame shapes them,
and they fight with icy cheekbones, with their mouths,
and turn whatever they attack into memories of ash.

TIMOTHY BALAND

Para el muro de un hospital de sangre

I.

Por los campos luchados se extienden los heridos.
Y de aquella extensión de cuerpos luchadores
salta un trigal de chorros calientes, extendidos
en roncos surtidores.

La sangre llueve siempre boca arriba, hacia el cielo.
Y las heridas suenan igual que caracolas,
cuando hay en las heridas celeridad de vuelo,
esencia de las olas.

La sangre huele a mar, sabe a mar y a bodega.
La bodega del mar, del vino bravo, estalla
allí donde el herido palpitante se anega,
y florece y se halla.

Herido estoy, miradme: necesito más vidas.
La que contengo es poca cosa para el gran cometido
de sangre que quisiera perder por las heridas.
Decid quién no fue herido.

Mi vida es una herida de juventud dichosa.
¡Ay de quién no esté herido, de quién jamás se siente
herido por la vida, ni en la vida reposa
herido alegremente!

Si hasta a los hospitales se va con alegría,
se convierten en huertos de heridas entreabiertas,
de adelfos florecidos ante la cirugía
de ensangrentadas puertas.

THE WOUNDED MAN

for the wall of a hospital in the front lines

I.

The wounded stretch out across the battlefields.
And from that stretched field of bodies that fight
a wheat-field of warm fountains springs up and spreads
    out
into streams with husky voices.

Blood always rains upward toward the sky.
And the wounds lie there making sounds like seashells,
if inside the wounds there is the swiftness of flight,
essence of waves.

Blood smells like the sea, and tastes like the sea, and the
    winecellar.
The wine cellar of the sea, of rough wine, breaks open
where the wounded man drowns, shuddering,
and he flowers and finds himself where he is.

I am wounded: look at me: I need more lives.
The one I have is too small for the consignment
of blood that I want to lose through wounds.
Tell me who has not been wounded.

My life is a wound with a happy childhood.
Pity the man who is not wounded, who doesn't feel
wounded by life, and never sleeps in life,
joyfully wounded.

If a man goes toward the hospitals joyfully,
they change into gardens of half-opened wounds,
of flowering oleanders in front of the surgery room
with its bloodstained doors.

II.

Para la libertad, sangro, lucho, pervivo,
Para la libertad, mis ojos y mis manos,
como un árbol carnal, generoso y cautivo,
doy a los cirujanos.

Para la libertad siento más corazones
que arenas en mi pecho: dan espumas mis venas,
y entro en los hospitales, y entro en los algodones
como en las azucenas.

Para la libertad me desprendo a balazos
de los que han revolcado su estatua por el lodo.
Y me desprendo a golpes de mis pies, de mis brazos,
de mi casa, de todo.

Porque donde unas cuencas vacías amanezcan,
ella pondrá dos piedras de futura mirada
y hará que nuevos brazos y nuevas piernas crezcan
en la carne talada.

Retoñarán aladas de savia sin otoño
reliquias de mi cuerpo que pierdo en cada herida.
Porque soy como el árbol talado, que retoño:
porque aún tengo la vida.

II.

Thinking of freedom I bleed, struggle, manage to live on.
Thinking of freedom, like a tree of blood
that is generous and imprisoned, I give my eyes and
    hands
to the surgeons.

Thinking of freedom I feel more hearts than grains of
    sand
in my chest: my veins give up foam,
and I enter the hospitals and I enter the rolls of gauze
as if they were lilies.

Thinking of freedom I break loose in battle
from those who have rolled her statue through the mud.
And I break loose from my feet, from my arms,
from my house, from everything.

Because where some empty eye-pits dawn,
she will place two stones that see into the future,
and cause new arms and new legs to grow
in the lopped flesh.

Bits of my body I lose in every wound
will sprout once more, sap-filled, autumnless wings.
Because I am like the lopped tree, and I sprout again:
because I still have my life.

JAMES WRIGHT

I.

Tened presente el hambre: recordad su pasado
turbio de capataces que pagaban en plomo.
Aquel jornal al precio de la sangre cobrado,
con yugos en el alma, con golpes en el lomo.

El hambre paseaba sus vacas exprimidas,
sus mujeres resecas, sus devoradas ubres,
sus ávidas quijadas, sus miserables vidas
frente a los comedores y los cuerpos salubres.

Los años de abundancia, la saciedad, la hartura
eran sólo de aquellos que se llamaban amos.
Para que venga el pan justo a la dentadura
del hambre de los pobres aqui estoy, aquí estamos.

Nosotros no podemos ser ellos, los de enfrente,
los que entienden la vida por un botín sangriento:
como los tiburones, voracidad y diente,
panteras deseosas de un mundo siempre hambriento.

Años del hambre han sido para el pobre sus años.
Sumaban para el otro su cantidad los panes.
Y el hambre alobadaba sus rapaces rebaños
de cuervos, de tenazas, de lobos, de alacranes.

Hambrientamente lucho yo, con todas mis brechas,
cicatrices y heridas, señales y recuerdos
del hambre, contra tantas barrigas satisfechas:
cerdos con un origen peor que el de los cerdos.

Por haber engordado tan baja y brutalmente,
más abajo de donde los cerdos se solazan,
seréis atravesados por esta gran corriente
de espigas que llamean, de puños que amenazan.

HUNGER

I.

Keep hunger in mind: remember its past
trampled with foremen who pay you in lead.
That wage is paid in blood received,
with a yoke on the soul, and blows to the back.

Hunger paraded its caved-in cows,
its dried-up women, its devoured teats,
its gaping jawbones, its miserable lives
past the strapping bodies of all the eaters.

The abundant years, the satiety, the glut
were only for those who get called boss.
I am here, we are here, to make sure that bread
goes straight to the teeth of the hungry poor.

Maybe we can't be those at the front
who understand life as bloody war-booty:
like sharks, all greed and tooth,
or eager panthers in a world always starving.

Years of hunger have been, for the poor, the only years.
Quantities of bread were heaped up for others,
and hunger wolfed down its ravenous flocks
of crows, clawed things, wolves, scorpions.

I fight, famished, will all my gashes,
scars, and wounds, souvenirs and memories
of hunger, against all those smug bellies:
hogs who were born more lowly than hogs.

For having gorged yourselves so basely and brutally,
wallowing deeper than pigs at play,
you will be plunged into this huge current
of blazing spikes, of menacing fists.

No habéis querido oír con orejas abiertas
el llanto de millones de niños jornaleros.
Ladrábais cuando el hambre llegaba a vuestras puertas
a pedir con la boca de los mismos luceros.

En cada casa, un odio como una higuera fosca,
como un tremante toro con los cuernos tremantes,
rompe por los tejados, os cerca y os embosca,
y os destruye a cornadas, perros agonizantes.

II.

El hambre es el primero de los conocimientos:
tener hambre es la cosa primera que se aprende.
Y la ferocidad de nuestros sentimientos,
allá donde el estómago se origina, se enciende.

Uno no es tan humano que no estrangule un día
pájaros sin sentir herida la conciencia:
que no sea capaz de ahogar en nieve fría
palomas que no saben si no es de la inocencia.

El animal influye sobre mí con extremo,
la fiera late en todas mis fuerzas, mis pasiones.
A veces, he de hacer un esfuerzo supremo
para acallar en mi la voz de los leones.

Me enorgullece el titulo de animal en mi vida,
pero en el animal humano persevero.
Y busco por mí cuerpo lo más puro que anida,
bajo tanta maleza, con su valor primero.

Por hambre vuelve el hombre sobre los laberintos
donde la vida habita siniestramente sola.
Reaparece la fiera, recobra sus instintos,
sus patas erizadas, sus rencores, su cola.

You have not wanted to open your ears to hear
the weeping of millions of young workers.
You just pay lip service, when hunger comes to the door
begging with the mouths of the very stars.

In every house: hatred, like a grove of fig trees,
like a quaking bull with shaking horns
breaking loose from the barn, circling, waiting,
and doing you in on its horns as you agonize like dogs.

II.

Hunger is the most important thing to know:
to be hungry is the first lesson we learn.
And the ferocity of what you feel,
there where the stomach begins, sets you on fire.

You aren't quite human if, when you strangle
doves one day you don't have a bad conscience:
if you can't drown doves in cold snow,
who know nothing, if not innocence.

The animal is a huge influence on me,
a beast roars through all my strength, my passions.
Sometimes I have to make the greatest effort
to calm the voice of the lion in me.

I am proud to own the animal in my life,
but in the animal, the human persists.
And I look for my body as the purest thing
to nest in such a jungle, with its basic courage.

Through hunger, man re-enters the labyrinth
where life is lived sinister, and alone.
The beast turns up again, recaptures its instincts,
its bristling paws, its animus, its tail.

Arroja los estudios y la sabiduría,
y se quita la máscara, la piel de la cultura,
los ojos de la ciencia, la corteza tardía
de los conocimientos que descubre y procura.

Entonces sólo sabe del mal, del exterminio.
Inventa gases, lanza motivos destructores,
regrese a la pezuña, retrocede al dominio
del colmillo, y avanza sobre los comedores.

Se ejercita en la bestia, y empuña la cuchara
dispuesto a que ninguno se le acerque a la mesa.
Entonces sólo veo sobre el mundo una piara
de tigres, y en mis ojos la visión duele y pesa.

Yo no tengo en el alma tanto tigre admitido,
tanto chacal prohijada, que el vino que me toca,
el pan, el día, el hambre no tenga compartido
con otras hambres puestas noblemente en la boca.

Ayudadme a ser hombre: no me dejéis ser fiera
hambrienta, encarnizada, sitiada eternamente.
Yo, animal familiar, con esta sangre obrera
os doy la humanidad que mi canción presiente.

Learning and wisdom are thrown out,
your mask is removed, the skin of culture,
the eyes of science, the recent crust
of knowledge that reveals and procures things.

Then you know only evil, extermination.
You invent gases, launch ruinous ideas,
return to the cloven hoof, regress to the kingdom
of the fang, dominate the big eaters.

You train the beast, clutch the ladle,
ready for anybody who comes near the table.
Then I see over the whole world only a troop
of tigers, and the sorry sight aches in my eyes.

I haven't opened my soul to so much tiger,
adopted so much of the jackal, that the wine I feel,
the bread, the day, the hunger isn't shared
with other hungers fed nobly into my mouth.

Help me to be a man: don't let me be a beast,
starving, enraged, forever cornered.
A common animal, with working blood,
I give you the humanity that this song foretells.

DON SHARE

El palomar de las cartas
abre su imposible vuelo
desde las trémulas mesas
donde se apoya el recuerdo,
la gravedad de la ausencia,
el corazón, el silencio.

Oigo un latido de cartas
navegando hacia su centro.

Donde voy, con las mujeres
y con los hombres me encuentro,
malheridos por la ausencia,
desgastados por el tiempo.

Cartas, relaciones, cartas:
tarjetas postales, sueños,
fragmentos de la ternura
proyectados en el cielo,
lanzados de sangre a sangre
y de deseo en deseo.

Aunque bajo la tierra
mi amante cuerpo esté,
escríbeme a la tierra,
que yo te escribiré.

En un rincón enmudecen
cartas viejas, sobres viejos,
con el color de la edad
sobre la escritura puesto.
Allí perecen las cartas
llenas de estremecimientos.
Allí agoniza la tinta
y desfallecen los pliegos,
y el papel se agujerea

The pigeon-house of letters
begins its impossible flight
from the trembling tables
where memory leans,
the weight of absence,
the heart, the silence.

I hear the wingbeat of letters
sailing toward their fate.

Wherever I go, I meet
women, men
badly wounded by absence,
withered by time.

Letters, stories, letters:
postcards, dreams,
fragments of tenderness
hurled into the sky,
sent from blood to blood,
from longing to longing.

Although my loving body
is under the earth now,
write to me on earth,
so I can write to you.

In the corner old letters,
old envelopes grow mute
with the color of age
pressed down on the writing.
There the letters perish
filled with shivering.
There the ink feels death throes,
and the loose sheets fail,
and the paper fills with holes

como un breve cementerio
de las pasiones de antes,
de los amores de luego.

Aunque bajo la tierra
mi amante cuerpo esté,
escribeme a la tierra,
que yo te escribiré.

Cuando te voy a escribir
se emocionan los tinteros:
los negros tinteros fríos
se ponen rojos y trémulos,
y un claro calor humano
sube desde el fondo negro.
Cuando te voy a escribir,
te van a escribir mis huesos:
te escribo con la imborrable
tinta de mi sentimiento.

Allá va mi carta cálida,
paloma forjada al fuego,
con las dos alas plegadas
y la dirección en medio.
Ave que sólo persigue,
para nido y aíre y cielo,
carne, manos, ojos tuyos,
y el espacio de tu aliento.

Y te quedarás desnuda
dentro de tus sentimientos,
sin ropa, para sentirla
del todo contra tu pecho.

Aunque bajo la tierra,
mi amante cuerpo esté,
escríbeme a la tierra,
que yo te escribiré.

like a small cemetery
of passions gone by,
of loves to come.

Although my loving body
is under the earth now,
write to me on earth,
so I can write to you.

When I'm about to write you
the inkwells stir,
those cold black wells
blush and tremble,
and a clear human warmth
rises from the black depths.
When I start to write you,
my bones start to write you:
I write with the indelible
ink of my love.

There goes my warm letter,
a pigeon forged in fire,
its two wings folded
and the address in the center.
Bird that only homes in
on its nest and air and sky,
your flesh, hands, eyes,
and the space of your breath.

And you will stay naked
inside your feelings,
without clothes, so you can feel
it all against your breast.

Although my loving body
is under the earth now,
write to me on earth,
so I can write to you.

Ayer se quedó una carta
abandonada y sin dueño,
volando sobre los ojos
de alguien que perdió su cuerpo.
Cartas que se quedan vivas
hablando para los muertos:
papel anhelante, humano,
sin ojos que puedan serlo.

Mientras los colmillos crecen,
cada vez más cerca siento
la leve voz de tu carta
igual que un clamor inmenso.
La recibiré dormido,
si no es posible despierto.
Y mis heridas serán
los derramados tinteros,
las bocas estremecidas
de rememorar tus besos,
y con su inaudita voz
han de repetir: *te quiero.*

Yesterday a letter was left
abandoned and unclaimed,
flying over the eyes
of someone who had lost his body.
Letters that stay alive
talking for the dead:
wistful paper, human,
without eyes to look at it.

While the eye-teeth keep growing,
I feel the gentle voice
of your letter grow
closer to an immense clamor.
It will come while I sleep,
if I can't stay awake.
And my wounds will be
the spilled inkwells,
the quivering mouths
that remember your kisses,
and with a voice no one hears
they will repeat: *I love you.*

TED GENOWAYS

I.

Las cárceles se arrastran por la humedad del mundo,
van por la tenebrosa vía de los juzgados:
buscan a un hombre, buscan a un pueblo, lo persiguen,
lo absorben, se lo tragan.

No se ve, no se escucha la pena de metal,
el sollozo del hierro que atropellan y escupen:
el llanto de la espada puesta sobre los jueces
de cemento fangoso.

Allí, bajo la cárcel, la fábrica del llanto,
el telar de la lágrima que no ha de ser estéril,
el casco de los odios y de las esperanzas,
fabrican, tejen, hunden.

Cuando están las perdices más roncas y acopladas,
y el azul amoroso de las fuerzas expansivas,
un hombre hace memoria de la luz, de la tierra,
húmedamente negro.

Se da contra las piedras la libertad, el día,
el paso galopante de un hombre, la cabeza,
la boca con espuma, con decisión de espuma,
la libertad, un hombre.

Un hombre que cosecha y arroja todo el viento
desde su corazón donde crece un plumaje:
un hombre que es el mismo dentro de cada frío,
de cada calabozo.

Un hombre que ha soñado con las aguas del mar,
y destroza sus alas como un rayo amarrado,
y estremece las rejas, y se clava los dientes
en los dientes del trueno.

THE PRISONS

I.

Prisons crawl through the dank of the world,
go on the tenebrous roads of the courts:
they look for a village, for a man, pursue him,
absorb him, swallow him.

You can't see, can't hear the metal punishment,
the iron sob of their trampling and spitting:
the lament of the sword held over the judges
of murky cement.

There, under the prison, the factory of laments,
the loom of tears that never finds itself bare,
the shell of hatreds and of hopes,
manufacture, weave, and sink.

When the partridges are hoarsest and coupled,
and the amorous blue of expansive forces,
a man has only his memory of light, of the earth,
dankly black.

Freedom crashes against stones, the day,
the galloping step of a man, the head,
the mouth of foam, with a decision of foam,
the freedom, a man.

A man who grasps and throws all the wind
from his heart where a plumage grows:
a man, the same man within each cold,
of each jail.

A man who has dreamed about waters of the sea,
and destroys his wings like a moored ray of light,
and shakes the grates, and sets his jaw
in the jaws of the thunder.

II.

Aquí no se pelea por un buey desmayado,
sino por un caballo que ve pudrir sus crines,
y siente sus galopes debajo de los cascos
pudrirse airadamente.

Limpiad el salivazo que lleva en la mejilla,
y desencadenad el corazón del mundo,
y detened las fauces de las voraces cárceles
donde el sol retrocede.

La libertad se pudre desplumada en la lengua
de quienes son sus siervos más que sus poseedores.
Romped esas cadenas, y las otras que escucho
detrás de esos esclavos.

Esos que sólo buscan abandonar su cárcel,
su rincón, su cadena, no la de los demás.
Y en cuanto lo consiguen, descienden pluma a pluma,
en mohecen, se arrastran.

Son los encadenados por siempre desde siempre.
Ser libre es una cosa que sólo un hombre sabe:
sólo el hombre que advierto dentro de esa mazmorra
como si yo estuviera.

Cierra las puertas, echa la aldaba, carcelero.
Ata duro a ese hombre: no le atarás el alma.
Son muchas llaves, muchos cerrojos, injusticias:
no le atarás el alma.

Cadenas, sí: cadenas de sangre necesita.
Hierros venenosos, cálidos, sanguíneos eslabones,
nudos que no rechacen a los nudos siguientes
humanamente atados.

II.

No one here fights for an ox without heart,
but for a horse who sees his own mane rotting away,
and feels his galloping rotting angrily
under his hooves.

Wipe away the lather that trails from his jaws
and take the chains off the heart of the world:
plug up the gullets of the greedy jails
where the sun backs away.

Freedom rots, molted on the tongue
of those who are serfs of freedom, not men.
Smash those chains, and the others I hear dragging
behind these slaves.

Those who only want to get out of their own prison,
their corner, their leg cuffs, and forget all the rest.
That done and over, they disintegrate feather by feather,
they start to mildew, they crawl.

They will be in chains forever and ever.
To be free is something only a man understands:
only the man I see locked underground
as if I were there.

Warden, shut the doors, slip in the crossbar.
Really tie him up: you won't tie his soul.
There are many keys, many locks, many unjust things:
you won't tie his soul.

Chains, yes: chains of blood are what he needs,
hunks of iron with veins, hot arterial links,
blood splices that will not exclude the later splices,
humanly made.

Un hombre aguarda dentro de un pozo sin remedio,
tenso, conmocionado, con la oreja aplicada.
Porque un pueblo ha gritado ¡libertad!, vuela el cielo.
Y las cárceles vuelan.

A man waits in a hole, no one to help,
tense, disturbed, his ear to the wall.
Because a people once cried out, Freedom! the heaven
    flies,
and the prison cells fly.

TED GENOWAYS, TIMOTHY BALAND, AND ROBERT BLY

Es sangre, no granizo, lo que azota mis sienes.
Son dos años de sangre: son dos inundaciones.
Sangre de acción solar, devoradora vienes,
hasta dejar sin nadie y ahogados los balcones.

Sangre que es el mejor de los mejores bienes.
Sangre que atesoraba para el amor sus dones.
Vedla enturbiando mares, sobrecogiendo trenes,
desalentando toros donde alentó leones.

El tiempo es sangre. El tiempo circula por mis venas.
Y ante el reloj y el alba me siento más que herido,
y oigo un chocar de sangres de todos los tamaños.

Sangre donde se puede bañar la muerte apenas:
fulgor emocionante que no ha palidecido,
porque lo recogieron mis ojos de mil años.

It is blood. It is not hail, battering my temples.
It is two years of blood; two enormous bloods.
Blood that acts like the sun, you come devouring,
till all the balconies are left drowned and empty.

Blood that is the best of all riches.
Blood that stored up its gifts for love.
See it stirring up seas, surprising trains,
breaking bulls' spirits as it heartens lions.

Time is blood. Time circulates through my veins.
In the presence of the clock and daybreak, I am more
    than wounded,
and I hear blood colliding, of every shape and size.

Blood where even death could hardly bathe:
moving brilliance of blood that has not grown pale,
because my eyes, a thousand years old, have given it
    shelter.

JAMES WRIGHT

Silencio que naufraga en el silencio
de las bocas cerradas de la noche.
No cesa de callar ni atravesado.
Habla el lenguaje ahogado de los muertos.

Silencio.

Abre caminos de algodón profundo,
amordaza las ruedas, los relojes,
detén la voz del mar, de la paloma:
emociona la noche de los sueños.

Silencio.

El tren lluvioso de la sangre suelta,
el frágil tren de los que se desangran,
el silencioso, el doloroso, el pálido,
el tren callado de los sufrimientos.

Silencio.

Tren de la palidez mortal que asciende:
la palidez reviste las cabezas,
el ¡ay! la voz, el corazón, la tierra,
el corazón de los que malhirieron.

Silencio.

Van derramando piernas, brazos, ojos,
van arrojando por el tren pedazos.
Pasan dejando rastros de amargura,
otra vía láctea de estelares miembros.

Silencio.

Ronco tren desmayado, envejecido:
agoniza el carbón, suspira el humo

Silence that shipwrecks in the silence
of the closed mouths during the night.
It never stops being silent, even when cut across.
It speaks the drowned language of the dead.

Silence.

Open the roads of deep cotton,
muffle the wheels, the clocks,
hold back the voice of the sea, of the pigeons:
stir up the night of dreams.

Silence.

The soaked train of escaping blood,
the frail train of men bleeding to death,
the silent, the painful train, the pale train,
the speechless train of agonies.

Silence.

Train of the deathly pallor that is ascending:
the pallor dresses the head,
the "ah!," the voice, the heart, the dust,
the heart of those who were badly wounded.

Silence.

They go, spilling legs, arms, eyes,
they go, throwing chunks through the train.
They pass, leaving bitter traces,
a new Milky Way, with their own members for stars.

Silence.

Hoarse train, disheartened, blood-red:
the coal lies in its last agony, the smoke heavily breathes,

y maternal la máquina suspira,
avanza con un largo desaliento.

Silencio.

Detenerse quisiera bajo un túnel
la larga madre, sollozar tendida.
No hay estaciones donde detenerse,
si no es el hospital, si no es el pecho.

Silencio.

Para vivir, con un pedazo basta:
en un rincón de carne cabe un hombre.
Un dedo sólo, un trozo sólo de ala
alza el vuelo total de todo un cuerpo.

Silencio.

Detened ese tren agonizante
que nunca acaba de cruzar la noche.
Y se queda descalzo hasta el caballo,
y enarena los cascos y el aliento.

and, maternal, the engine sighs,
it moves on, like a long discouragement.

Silence.

The long mother would like to come to a stop
under a tunnel, and lie down weeping.
There are no way stations for us,
except in the hospital, or else in the breast.

Silence.

To live, a mere bit is enough:
in a single corner of flesh, you can put up a man.
One finger alone, one piece of a wing alone
can lift the whole body into absolute flight.

Silence.

Stop that dying train
that never completes its journey across the night.
Even the dying horse is left without shoes,
and the hooves, and the breath, are buried under the
    sand.

JAMES WRIGHT

Abrazado a tu cuerpo como el tronco a su tierra,
con todas las raíces y todos los corajes,
¿quién me separará, me arrancará de ti,
madre?

Abrazado a tu vientre, ¿quién me lo quitará,
si su fondo titánico da principio a mi carne?
Abrazado a tu vientre, que es mi perpetua casa,
¡nadie!

Madre: abismo de siempre, tierra de siempre: entrañas
donde desembocando se unen todas las sangres:
donde todos los huecos caídos se levantan:
madre.

Decir madre es decir *tierra que me ha parido;*
es decir a los muertos: *hermanos, levantarse;*
es sentir en la boca y escuchar bajo el suelo
sangre.

La otra madre es un puente, nada más, de tus ríos.
El otro pecho es una burbuja de tus mares.
Tú eres la madre entera con todo su infinito,
madre.

Tierra: tierra en la boca, y en el alma, y en todo.
Tierra que voy comiendo, que al fin ha de tragarme.
Con más fuerza que antes volverás a parirme,
madre.

Cuando sobre tu cuerpo sea una leve huella,
volverás a parirme con más fuerza que antes.
Cuando un hijo es un hijo, vive y muere gritando:
¡madre!

Hugging your body like a trunk hugs the earth,
with all the roots and all the angers;
who will separate me, will uproot me from you,
mother?

Hugging your womb, who will remove me,
if its titanic depth gives essence to my flesh?
Hugging your womb, that is my perpetual house,
nobody!

Mother: abyss of always, land of always: entrails
where in the end all the bloods are united:
where all the fallen hollows rise:
mother.

To say mother is to say *earth that has given birth to me;*
it is to say to the dead: *brothers, arise;*
it is to feel in the mouth and to hear under the ground
blood.

The other mother is a bridge, nothing else, of your rivers.
The other heart is a bubble in your seas.
You are the whole mother in all your infinity,
mother.

Earth: earth in the mouth, and the soul, and everything.
Earth that I am eating, that finally has to swallow me.
With more force than before, you will return to give birth
    to me,
mother.

When I am but a slight trace upon your body,
you will return to give birth to me with more force than
    before.
When a son is a son, lives and dies shouting:
mother!

Hermanos: defendamos su vientre acometido,
hacia donde los grajos crecen de todas partes,
pues, para que las malas alas vuelen, aún quedan
aires.

Echad a las orillas de vuestro corazón
el sentimiento en límites, los afectos parciales.
Son pequeñas historias al lado de ella, siempre
grande.

Una fotografía y un pedazo de tierra,
una carta y un monte son a veces iguales.
Hoy eres tú la hierba que crece sobre todo,
madre.

Familia de esta tierra que nos funde en la luz,
los más oscuros muertos pugnan por levantarse,
fundirse con nosotros y salvar la primera
madre.

España, piedra estoica que se abrió en dos pedazos
de dolor y de piedra profunda para darme:
no me separarán de tus altas entrañas,
madre.

Además de morir por ti, pido una cosa:
que la mujer y el hijo que tengo, cuando pasen,
vayan hasta el rincón que habite de tu vientre,
madre.

Brothers: let us defend her besieged womb,
against the crows increasing everywhere,
while, for their evil wings to fly, there are still
breezes.

Consign to the borders of your heart
limited feelings, the partial affections.
They are but gossip next to her, always
great.

A photograph and a piece of earth,
a letter and a mountain are sometimes equal.
Today you are the grass that grows over everything,
mother.

Family of this earth that fuses us into the light,
the darkest dead struggle to rise,
to be fused with us and to save the first
mother.

Spain, stoic stone that was opened in two pieces
to give me pain and deeper stone:
they will not separate me from your deep entrails,
mother.

Besides to die by you, I request one thing:
that the woman and the son I have, when they pass,
will go to the corner where I live in your womb,
mother.

TED GENOWAYS

Pintada, no vacía:
pintada está mi casa
del color de las grandes
pasiones y desgracias.

Regresará del llanto
adonde fue llevada
con su desierta mesa,
con su ruinosa cama.

Florecerán los besos
sobre las almohada.

Y en torno de los cuerpos
elevará la sábana
su inmensa enredadera
nocturna, perfumada.

El odio se amortigua
detrás de la ventana.

Será la garra suave.

Dejadme la esperanza.

LAST SONG

Painted, not empty:
my house is painted
the color of the great
passions and tragedies.

It will return from the flood of tears
where it was carried
with its deserted table,
with its ruined bed.

Kisses will flower
on the pillows.

And wrapped around the bodies
the sheet will raise
its intense vine,
nocturnal, perfumed.

Hatred dies down
outside the window.

The claw will be tender.

Leave me this hope.

TED GENOWAYS

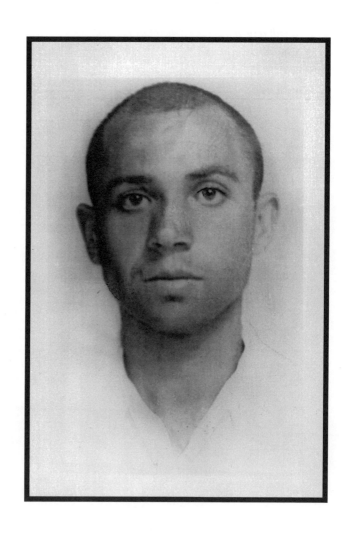

THE PRISON POEMS: 1939–1942

The First Imprisonment

Despite his severe beating and incarceration for attempting to seek polit-
ical asylum in Portugal, Miguel Hernández expected a short stay in Tor-
rijos Prison. His friend and former employer José María de Cossío was
an influential man in Madrid, a man he felt confident could "help me to
leave quickly."[1] On May 18, 1939, still suffering from internal injuries, he
sent Josefina a postcard:

> I'm in Torrijos 65, not in good health, but still I am here. If I
> could have written to you sooner I would have done it. I
> knew you would be worried. Take heart, because soon I will
> be at your side.[2]

By the end of May, his optimism had waned and Hernández began to
send names of people for Josefina to contact and inform of his situa-
tion—Vicente Aleixandre, Luis Almarcha, Juan Bellod. Cossío had been
able to visit him—even to get him chocolate, cheese, and preserves—
but he was not able to secure so much as a provisional liberty for
Hernández.

With the end of June approaching, Hernández wrote to Neruda, who
was by then in Paris making arrangements for Spanish Loyalists—espe-
cially artists—to receive political asylum in Chile. Having heard of these
efforts, Hernández implored him to come to his aid, as he had years be-
fore when Hernández was arrested in Jarama:

> Perhaps . . . through your country's Embassy in Madrid,
> where I have found myself detained for several months, you
> know of me and what situation I am in. It is an absolute ne-
> cessity that you do whatever is in your power to secure my
> exit from Spain and the arrival on your soil in the shortest
> space of time possible.[3]

1. Letter to Cossío, May 20, 1939. Hernández, *Obra completa,* 3: 2540–2541.
2. Hernández, *Obra completa,* 3: 2540.
3. Ibid., 2548.

Deprived by the prison guards of the photographs he constantly begged Josefina to send of his infant son, often going weeks without word from any family, and now receiving no reply from Neruda, Hernández slumped into despair as the summer drew to its close. Worse yet, when he did hear from Josefina, he was tormented by the news that she had only onions and bread to eat. He feared that his son, his little Manolo, would die from the same malnutrition that had claimed his other son. A letter dated September 12, 1939, accompanied by what is now Hernández's best-known poem, "Nanas de la Cebolla" ("Lullabies of the Onion"), presages the despair that pervades Hernández's prison poems:

> These days I have been thinking about your situation, each day more difficult. The smell of the onion you are eating reaches me here and my child must feel indignant about having to suck and draw out onion juice instead of milk. To console you I send some verse that I have done, since I have no other task but to write you or despair. I prefer the former, so I do only that, besides washing and sewing with extreme seriousness and agility, as if I had done nothing else in my life. Also I spend time purging myself of a tiny family which I'm never free of, and at times I breed it robust and big like a chickpea. It will all be over with by means of fighting and patience—or they, the lice, will finish me off. But they are too small a thing for me, brave as always, and even if these bugs that want to carry off my blood were elephants, I would wipe them from the map of my body. Poor body! Between scabies, lice, bedbugs and every kind of animal vermin, without freedom, without you, Josefina, and without you, Manolillo of my soul, I don't know at times what attitude to take, and finally, I decide on hope, which I never lose.[4]

Unknown to Hernández, Neruda was working furiously on his behalf. Years later, in the Chilean magazine *Ercilla*, Neruda wrote of his efforts to secure Hernández's release in late summer 1939:

> At a P. E. N. club meeting in Paris I talked with María Teresa León (the wife of Rafael Alberti) and with the French poetess Marie-Anne Conméne. María Teresa remembered that Hernández had been a Catholic poet and that he had

4. Barnstone, 272–273.

written a religious play called *Who Has Seen You and Sees You Still*. Marie-Anne immediately started hunting all over Paris for a copy of the play. Finally we found one, which was then given to the Cardinal Baudrillart to read, since he spoke Spanish and was a good friend of Franco. By then the Cardinal was entirely blind, but the play was read to him. He was so impressed that he immediately petitioned Franco for Hernández's freedom. That's how Miguel got out of prison.

Then he went over to the Chilean embassy, in order to pick up his visa and leave for Chile. It was a mistake. The Charge d'Affaires then was Carlos Morla Lynch,[5] who denied him asylum . . . because he had written poems insulting to General Franco. From Madrid Miguel wrote me a last letter, in which he explained in his simple way that he hoped to come to my country and become a Chilean citizen.[6] He left Madrid for Orihuela, to look for his wife and baby son.[7]

Though all of his friends warned him against returning home, Hernández was desperate to see his wife and child. He had no intention of fleeing to Chile without them. When his train stopped in Alicante, his relatives, townspeople, even the mayor, came to the station to beg him not to go to Orihuela. Hernández would not be swayed. On his arrival in his hometown, Josefina and Manolo greeted him at the station and took him to the house of Gabriel Sijé for dinner. They stayed there together for nearly two weeks. Hernández had with him a notebook of seventy-nine poems composed from October 1938 up to "Lullabies of the Onion," written barely a week before. On the cover he had written *Cancionero y romancero de ausencias*, literally *Songbook and Balladbook of Absences*. While at the Sijé home, he gave the notebook to Josefina for safekeeping, but from the few letters Hernández wrote there, it seems clear that he did not fear imminent arrest. He even wrote to José María de Cossío, hoping to renew his interest in publishing an anthology of

5. A Chilean playwright whose account of these events appears in *Memoria presentada al Gobierno de Chile correspondiente a mi labor al frente de nuestra Embajada en Madrid: Durante la guerra civil, 1937–1938–1939 (Report to the Chilean Government Concerning My Work as the Head of Our Embassy in Madrid: During the Spanish Civil War, 1937–1939.)*

6. Neruda appears to be thinking of the earlier quoted letter written by Hernández in June, not September.

7. Hernández and de Otero, *Selected Poems*, 108. Translation by Timothy Baland.

classical and romantic Spanish poetry. So Hernández must have been surprised on September 29, his saint's day, to have been arrested as he left the Sijé residence, and taken to a seminary converted into a prison in Orihuela.

The Second Imprisonment

Within days of his second incarceration, Hernández wrote Josefina a letter still fresh with his indignation and disbelief:

> In this place I feel worse off than in Madrid. No one there, not even those who got nothing through the mail, experienced the kind of hunger we have here, and so we never saw there the sort of faces and events and illnesses we see in this place. Our countrymen seem extremely interested in having me notice how mean-hearted they are, and since I fell into their hands I've been experiencing this. The thin-fingered ones will never forgive me for having placed my poetry, all the intelligence I have, and my unselfish heart—two things of course bigger than all of them put together—in the service of the people in a straightforward and open way. They'd prefer me to be an ordinary coward. They haven't succeeded in that yet, and they won't. My son is going to inherit from his father not money, but honor. But not the "honor" gained by lying and playing along with these worst types disguised as the best.[8]

He remained in the converted seminary until December 3, when he was transferred to the Madrid prison of Count of Toreno.

Six weeks later, January 18, 1940, Hernández was officially charged for the first time—along with over twenty other prisoners. That same day, he was brought before a makeshift tribunal to stand trial on charges of belonging to the Communist party, writing poems against Franco's nationalist forces, and for "contributing through deeds and words to the many crimes perpetrated in the red zone."[9] Hernández was appointed a

8. Ibid, 109.
9. Hernández, *Obra completa*, 1: 107.

lawyer who had been made aware of the charges only the day before. Hopelessly ill-prepared, he submitted a list of people willing to vouch for Hernández and then said only this:

> Miguel Hernández is a good poet, but he is an excellent person of arduous and proud temperament. In the summary there are guarantees and testimonials of some intellectuals, registered by José María de Cossío, whose identification with the Movement it is not possible to doubt, attesting to his perfect honorability. Against him there is nothing more than his political verses, his labor as the Commissar of Culture, and his ascription to Marxist communism: but no one has imputed him with any dishonest or bloody action.[10]

That fact notwithstanding, Hernández—and all the others who were tried—were sentenced to death. Over the next months, the majority were gunned down by firing squads within the prison walls. The propaganda wing of the new Fascist government issued a flier reading:

> Miguel Hernández, condemned to death.
> Crime: Poet and soldier of the mother country.
> Aggravating, intelligentsia.
> Death to the intelligentsia.[11]

Owing to pressure from the international community, however, and fearing a popular backlash like the one following Lorca's execution, the sentence was commuted to thirty years in prison. It was still a death sentence. In a letter dated May 6, 1940, written from Count of Toreno, he described the nightmarish conditions of the prison:

> For the last several nights the rats have taken to wandering over my body while I sleep. The other night I woke up and had one at the side of my mouth. This morning I caught another one in the sleeve of my pullover, and every day I have to pick their dung out of my hair. Seeing my head full of rat shit, I say to myself: So this is what I'm worth now! Even the rats come and leave dung on the roof of our thoughts. That's what is new in my life: rats. Now I have rats,

10. Ibid., 108.
11. Fonseca Fernández, 184.

lice, fleas, bedbugs, mange. . . . The corner I have for a home
will soon be a positive zoological garden, or, maybe, a wild
animal cage.[12]

Despite being subjected to the worst imaginable conditions and being
bounced from prison to prison through the fall, Hernández continued to
write poems, often scribbling them on stolen scraps of paper and smug-
gling them to friends. By now *Songbook and Balladbook of Absences* was
nearly complete, but soon Hernández's health began to fail. In the
provincial prison in Palencia that October, he suffered his first bout of
pneumonia, then bronchitis in Ocaña at the end of the harsh winter of
1940.

In the summer of 1941, he was transferred to the Adult Reformatory
of Alicante, very near his family, but by the winter of that year, he had
contracted tuberculosis. In February 1942, he wrote Josefina:

By means of a pointed apparatus placed in my side, after
looking at me again under X-rays, they took from my left
lung, without exaggeration, more than a liter and a half of
pus pouring out in a stream for more than ten minutes.[13]

It was clear that without proper medical attention, Hernández would
die. One of the doctors offered to arrange a transfer to a high-quality
clinic, but by the time permission was granted by the state, Hernández
was too ill to move. Instead, he was subjected to a stopgap prison sur-
gery, performed by Dr. Antonio Barbero. In an undated letter, written in
early spring, Hernández describes his suffering in excruciating detail:

Josefina, the hemorrhaging has stopped. But I have to tell
Dr. Barbero that the pus is not draining through the tube he
put in; instead, the opening has enlarged and the pus builds
up and then runs out on the bed, during a coughing fit
sometimes. This is a bother and interfering with my rate of
recovery. I want to get away from here as soon as I can. They
are trying to cure me by brilliant ideas off and on, and every-
thing is sloppiness and stupidity and couldn't-care-less.
Well, love, I do feel better. As soon as I get out of here, the

12. Hernández and de Otero, *Selected Poems*, 109–110. Translation by Timothy Ba-
land.

13. Hernández, *Obra completa*, 1: 109.

recovery will go like lightning. Kiss our son for me. I love you, Josefina.[14]

On March 27, 1942, Josefina was allowed to visit, but Hernández was heartbroken and sobbed that she had not brought Manolo, repeating inconsolably, "You should have brought him. You should have brought him."[15] Josefina later remembered:

> I returned to visit him the following day and when I put the bag of food on the floor, I was repelled by his eyes watching me. I left without saying anything. I didn't have the courage to be sure he was dead. . . . It was the 28th of March, a Saturday. The day before Palm Sunday.[16]

More than thirty years later, Pablo Neruda would write simply: "The nightingale could not survive in captivity."[17] When Miguel Hernández was found dead on his cot in the Alicante prison infirmary, on the wall above his bed were written his last lines of poetry:

> Adíos, brothers, comrades, friends,
> let me take leave of the sun and of the fields![18]

The eyes that had haunted Josefina with their vacant stare were still wide open and could not be closed. Though his final completed poem was entitled "Eterna Sombra" ("Eternal Darkness") and the theme of darkness dominated the last poems gathered in *Songbook and Balladbook of Absences*, his close friend Vicente Aleixandre said many years later of the dead poet: "The light never went out in him, not even in the last moment, the light that, more than anything else, made him die tragically with his eyes open."[19]

14. Hernández and de Otero, *Selected Poems*, 110. Translation by Timothy Baland.
15. Hernández, *Obra completa*, 1: 111.
16. Ibid.
17. Neruda, 126, translated by St. Martin.
18. Quoted in Barnstone, 277.
19. Hernández and de Otero, *Selected Poems*, 138. Translation by Hardie St. Martin.

[CANCIONERO Y ROMANCERO DE AUSENCIAS]
(1941)

[SONGBOOK AND BALLADBOOK OF ABSENCES]
(1941)

6

El cementerio está cerca
de donde tú y yo dormimos,
entre nopales azules,
pitas azules y niños
que gritan vívidamente
si un muerto nubla camino.
De aquí al cementerio, todo
es azul, dorado, límpido.
Cuatro pasos, y los muertos.
Cuatro pasos, y los vivos.
Límpido, azul y dorado,
se hace allí remoto el hijo.

6

The cemetery lies near
where you and I are sleeping,
among blue prickly-pear,
blue century-plants and children
who cry out with such life
if a dead body throws its shadow on the road.
From here to the cemetery, everything
is blue, golden, clear.
Four steps and the dead.
Four steps and the living.
Clear, blue, and golden
my son, there, seems far away.

JAMES WRIGHT

8

¿Qué quiere el viento de encono
que baja por el barranco
y violenta las ventanas
mientras te visto de abrazos?

Derribarnos, arrastrarnos.

Derribadas, arrastradas,
las dos sangres se alejaron.
¿Qué sigue queriendo el viento
cada vez más enconado?

Separarnos.

8

[WHAT DOES THE BITTER WIND WANT]

What does the bitter wind want
that it comes down the ravine
and breaks through the windows
while I dress you in my arms?

To fell us. To drag us away.

Fallen, dragged down,
both bloods receded.
What else does the wind want
more bitter by the minute?

To separate us.

TED GENOWAYS

VALS DE LOS ENAMORADOS Y UNIDOS HASTA SIEMPRE

No salieron jamás
Del vergel del abrazo.
Y ante el rojo rosal
De los besos rodaron.

Huracanes quiesieron
Con rencor separarlos.
Y las hachas tajantes,
Y los rígidos rayos.

Aumentaron la tierra
De las pálidas manos.
Precipios midieron,
Por el viento impulsados
Entre bocas deshechas.
Recorrieron naufragios,
Cada vez más profundos
En sus cuerpos sus brazos.
Perseguidos, hundidos
Por un gran desamparo
De recuerdo y lunas,
De noviembre y marzos,
Aventados se vieron
Como polvo liviano:
Aventados se vieron,
Pero siempre abrazados.

WALTZ POEM OF THOSE IN LOVE AND INSEPARABLE FOREVER

They never left
the walled garden of their arms.
They wound in circles
about the red rosebush of the lips.

Storms tried to part them
out of pure spite;
so did hard-bitten axes
and bony lightning.

They added something good
to a land of pale hands.
Their bodies measured cliffs
being shoved along by wind
between crumbling mouths.
They rummaged through shipwreck after shipwreck,
their arms each time
growing deeper into their bodies.
Hunted down, crushed,
left alone and abandoned
by moons and memories,
Marches and Novembers,
they saw themselves whirled
like dust that counts for nothing:
they saw themselves whirled,
but they have each other's arms forever.

TIMOTHY BALAND

11

[COMO LA HIGUERA JOVEN]

Como la higuera joven
de los barrancos eras.
Y cuando yo pasaba
sonabas en la sierra.
Como la higuera joven,
resplandeciente y ciega.

Como la higuera eres.
Como la higuera vieja.
Y paso, y me saludan
silencio y hojas secas.

Como la higuera eres
que el rayo envejeciera.

11

[YOU WERE LIKE A YOUNG FIG TREE]

You were like a young fig tree
in the craggy cliffs.
And when I walked by
I heard you in the mountains.
Like the young fig tree,
glittering and blind.

You are like a fig tree.
Like an old fig tree.
I pass by and you greet me
with silence and dry leaves.

You are like a fig tree
made old by lightning.

TED GENOWAYS

12

El sol, la rosa y el niño
flores de un dîa nacieron.
Los de cada día son
soles, flores, niños nuevos.

Mañana no seré yo:
otro será el verdadero.
Y no seré más allá
de quien quiera su recuerdo.

Flor de un día es los más grande
al pie de lo más pequeño.
Flor de la luz el relámpago,
y flor del instante el tiempo.

Entre las flores te fuiste.
Entre las flores me quedo.

12

The sun, the rose, and the child
were born day-flowers.
Every day things are new
suns, new flowers, children.

Tomorrow I'll no longer be:
someone else will be real.
And I won't exist beyond
whoever desires the memory.

A day-flower is biggest
at the foot of what is smallest.
Flower of light the lightning,
flower of time the moment.

Among the flowers you went away.
Among the flowers I lag behind.

EDWIN HONIG

18

Cada vez que paso
bajo tu ventana,
me azota el aroma
que aún flota en tu casa.
Cada vez que paso
junto al cementerio
me arrastra la fuerza
que aún sopla en tus huesos.

18

[EACH TIME I PASS]

Each time I pass
under your window,
I am struck by the fragrance
that still floats through your house.
Each time I pass
by the cemetery
I am drawn back by the power
that still blows through your bones.

TED GENOWAYS

24

[*UNA FOTOGRAFÍA*]

Una fotografía.

Un cartón expresivo,
envuelto por los meses
en los rincones íntimos.

Un agua de distancia
quiero beber; gozar
un fondo de fantasma.
Un cartón me conmueve.

Un cartón me acompaña.

24

[A PHOTOGRAPH]

A photograph.

An expressive picture,
its intimate corners
curled by the months.

I want to drink from
a distant lake: to rejoice
in its phantom depths.
A picture disturbs me.

A picture accompanies me.

TED GENOWAYS

[LLEVADME AL CEMENTERIO]

Llevadme al cementerio
de los zapatos viejos.

Echadme a todas horas
la pluma de la escoba.

Sembradme con estatuas
de rígida mirada.

Por un huerto de bocas,
futuras y doradas,
relumbrará mi sombra.

33

[CARRY ME TO THE CEMETERY]

Carry me to the cemetery
of old shoes.

Throw me at all hours
the pen of the broom.

Sow me with statues
rigidly staring.

Through an orchard of mouths,
promising and golden,
my shadow will go glittering.

TED GENOWAYS

[LAS GRAMAS, LA ORTIGAS]

Las gramas, la ortigas
en el otoño avanzan
con una suavidad
y una ternura largas.

El otoño, un sabor
que separan las cosas
las aleja y arrastra.

Llueve sobre tejado
como sobre una caja
mientras la hierba crece
como una joven ala.

Las gramas, las ortigas
nutre una misma savia.

[GRASSBLADES, NETTLES]

Grassblades, nettles,
advance in autumn
with a long-drawn-out
smoothness and tenderness.

Autumn, a flavor
that separates things,
estranges them and pulls them along.

It rains down on the roof
like it rains down on a box
while grass grows up
like youthful wings.

The same energy nourishes
grassblades and nettles.

GARY J. SCHMECHEL

40

Todas las casas son ojos
que resplandecen y acechan.

Todas las casas son bocas
que escupen, muerden y besan.

Todas las casas son brazos
que se empujan y se estrechan.

De todas las casas salen
soplos de sombra y de selva.

En todas hay un clamor
de sangres insatisfechas.

Y a un grito todas las casas
se asaltan y se despueblan.

Y a un grito todas se aplacan,
y se fecundan, y esperan.

[ALL THE HOUSES ARE EYES]

All the houses are eyes
that gleam and watch.

All the houses are mouths
that spit, bite, and kiss.

All the houses are arms
that push away and hold on tight.

From each house come
gusts of shadow and of jungle.

In every one there's a cry
of unsatisfied blood.

And with a scream all the houses
attack each other and empty out.

And with a scream they grow calm,
and become fertile, and wait.

GARY J. SCHMECHEL

[*EL AMOR ASCENDÍA ENTRE NOSOTROS*]

El amor ascendía entre nosotros
como la luna entre las dos palmeras
que nunca se abrazaron.

El íntimo rumor de los dos cuerpos
hacia el arrullo un oleaje trajo,
pero la ronca voz fue atenazada.
Fueron pétreos los labios.

El ansia de ceñir movió la carne,
esclareció los huesos inflamados,
pero los brazos al querer tenderse
murieron en los brazos.

Pasó el amor, la luna, entre nosotros
y devoró los cuerpos solitarios.
Y somos dos fantasmas que se buscan
y se encuentran lejanos.

41

[LOVE CLIMBED BETWEEN US]

Love climbed between us
like the moon between two trees
that have never embraced.

The hidden murmur of our bodies
surged toward a lullaby,
but the voice was hoarse and tortured.
The lips were stone.

The longing to clasp aroused the flesh,
exalting the fevered bones,
but the arms, stretching out,
withered as they were.

Love passed between us like the moon
and devoured our lonely bodies.
And we are two ghosts who seek one another
and meet far off.

JOHN HAINES

43

Romorosas pestañas
de los cañaverales.
Cayendo sobre el sueño
del hombre hasta dejarle
el pecho apaciguado
y la cabeza suave.

Ahogad la voz del arma,
que no despierte y salte
con el cuchillo de odio
que entre sus dientes late.

Así, dormido, el hombre
toda la tierra vale.

[RUSTLING EYELASHES]

> Rustling eyelashes
> of the canefields.
> Falling over a man's
> dream until he is left
> with heart calmed
> and mind soothed.
>
> Drown the weapon's voice
> so it does not wake up and leap
> with hate's knife
> quivering between its teeth.
>
> In this way, sleeping, a man
> is worth the entire earth.

GARY J. SCHMECHEL

49

[LA VEJEZ DE LOS PUEBLOS]

La vejez de los pueblos.
El corazón sin dueño.
El amor sin objeto.
La hierba, el polvo, el cuervo.
¿Y la juventud?
En el ataúd.

El árbol solo y seco.
La mujer como un leño
de viudez sobre el lecho.
El odio sin remedio.
¿Y la juventud?
En el ataúd.

[THE AGED IN THE VILLAGES]

The aged in the villages.
The ownerless heart.
Affection without object.
The grass, the dust, the crow.
And youth?
In the coffin.

The tree alone and withered.
The woman like a log
of widowhood over the bed.
Hatred without remedy.
And youth?
In the coffin.

TED GENOWAYS

A MI HIJO

Te has negado a cerrar los ojos, muerto mío,
abiertos ante el cielo como dos golondrinas:
su color coronado de junios, ya es rocío
alejándose a ciertas regiones matutinas.

Hoy, que es un día como bajo la tierra, oscuro,
como bajo la tierra, lluvioso, despoblado,
con la humedad sin sol de mi cuerpo futuro,
como bajo la tierra quiero haberte enterrado.

Desde que tú eres muerto no alientan las mañanas,
al fuego arrebatadas de tus ojos solares:
precipitado octubre contra nuestras ventanas,
diste paso al otoño y anocheció los mares.

Te ha devorado el sol, rival único y hondo
y la remota sombra que te lanzó encendido;
te empuja luz abajo llevándote hasta el fondo,
tragándote; y es como si no hubieras nacido.

Diez meses en la luz, redondeando el cielo,
sol muerto, anochecido, sepultado, eclipsado.
Sin pasar por el día se marchitó tu pelo;
atardeció tu carne con el alba en un lado.

El pájaro pregunta por ti, cuerpo al oriente,
carne naciente al alba y al júbilo precisa;
niño que sólo supo reír, tan largamente,
que sólo ciertas flores mueren con tu sonrisa.

Ausente, ausente, ausente como la golondrina,
ave estival que esquiva vivir al pie del hielo:
golondrina que a poco de abrir la pluma fina,
naufraga en las tijeras enemigas del vuelo.

TO MY SON

You have refused to close your eyes, my dead one,
and they are open to the sky like two swallows:
your June-crowned color is now dew
drifting toward patches of morning light.

Today is like a day under the earth; it's dark,
rainy, deserted as if under earth,
damp, sunless as the corpse I will be,
like the earth I would like to have buried you under.

Since you died, mornings give no hope,
robbed of your fiery sun-lit eyes:
with October pressing against our windows,
you cleared autumn's path, turned seas into night.

The sun, your only rival, devoured you
deep as the distant shadow that set you ablaze;
light pulled you down, bore you to the bottom,
swallowed you; and it is as if you were never born.

Ten months in the light, with the dead sun
rounding the sky, blackened, entombed, eclipsed.
Without passing through daylight, your hair faded;
your flesh alongside dawn drew toward evening.

The bird, facing east, asks after you.
A newborn body needs the dawn and happiness,
my little child who knew only laughter, so much
that only certain flowers die with your smile.

Gone, gone, gone like the swallow,
summer bird that flees life touched by frost:
swallow who, just opening his delicate wings,
has them clipped, is stranded by the enemies of flight.

Flor que no fue capaz le endurecer los dientes,
de llegar al más leve signo de la fiereza.
Vida como una hoja de labios incipientes,
hoja que se desliza cuando a sonar empieza.

Los consejos del mar de nada te han valido . . .
Vengo de dar a un tierno sol una puñalada,
de enterrar un pedazo de pan en el olvido,
de echar sobre unos ojos un puñado de nada.

Verde, rojo, moreno; verde, azul y dorado;
los latentes colores de la vida, los huertos,
el centro de las flores a tus pies destinado,
de oscuros negros tristes, dc graves blancos yertos.

Mujer arrinconada: mira que ya es de día.
(¡Ay, ojos sin poniente por siempre en la alborada!)
Pero en tu vientre, pero en tus ojos, mujer mía,
la noche continúa cayendo desolada.

Flower too young to harden its teeth,
to muster the slightest sign of ferocity.
Life like the leaf of newborn lips,
a leaf that falls just as it starts to speak.

The sea's advice was worthless to you . . .
I've come to stab the tender sun,
to bury a slice of bread in oblivion,
to toss into those eyes a handful of nothing.

Green, red, brown; green, blue, gold;
the latent colors of life, gardens,
the insides of flowers destined for your feet,
and sad deep blacks, stiff grave whites.

Cornered woman: look, it's day now.
(Oh, eyes that never set on dawn!)
But in your womb, in your eyes, my wife,
desolate night keeps falling.

TED GENOWAYS

[TODO ESTÁ LLENO DE TI]

Todo está lleno de ti,
y todo de mí está lleno:
llenas están las ciudades,
igual que los cementerios

de ti, por todas las casas,
de mí, por todos los cuerpos.

Por las calles voy dejando
algo que voy recogiendo:
pedazos de vida mía
venidos desde muy lejos.

Voy alado a la agonía
arrastrándome me veo
en el umbral, en el fundo
latente de nacimiento.

Todo está lleno de mí:
de algo que es tuyo y recuerdo
perdido, pero encontrado
alguna vez, algún tiempo.

Tiempo que se queda atrás
decididamente negro,
indeleblemente rojo,
dorado sobre tu cuerpo.

Todo está lleno de ti,
traspasado de tu pelo:
de algo que no he conseguido
y que busco entre tus huesos.

54

[EVERYTHING IS FULL OF YOU]

Everything is full of you
and I am full of everything:
the cities are full,
and the cemeteries are full,

you, with all the houses,
me, with all the bodies.

Down the streets, I will leave
something that I will retake:
pieces of my life
come from far away.

I go, feathered by agony
against my will, to see myself
in the threshold, in the bottom
hidden since birth.

Everything is full of me:
of something that is yours and memory
lost, but found
once more, some day.

Days that linger behind
decidedly black,
indelibly red,
golden upon your body.

Cast from your hair,
everything is full of you:
of something that I haven't found
and look for among your bones.

TED GENOWAYS

59

[TRISTES GUERRAS]

Tristes guerras
si no es amor la empresa.
Tristes, tristes.

Tristes armas
si no son las palabras.
Tristes, tristes.

Tristes hombres
si no mueren de amores.
Tristes, tristes.

59

Sad wars
if love is not the aim.
Sad, sad.

Sad weapons
if they are not words.
Sad, sad.

Sad men
if they do not die for love.
Sad, sad.

TED GENOWAYS

I. *Hijo de la sombra*

Eres la noche, esposa: la noche en el instante
mayor de su potencia lunar y femenina.
Eres la medianoche: la sombra culminante
donde culmina el sueño, donde el amor culmina.

Forjado por el día, mi corazón que quema
lleva su gran pisada de sol adonde quieres,
con un solar impulso, con una luz suprema,
cumbre de las mañanas y los atardeceres.

Daré sobre tu cuerpo cuando la noche arroje
su avaricioso anhelo de imán y poderío.
Un astral sentimiento febril me sobrecoge,
incendía mí osamenta con un escalofrío.

El aire de la noche desordena tus pechos,
y desordena y vuelca los cuerpos con su choque.
Como una tempestad de enloquecidos lechos,
eclipsa las parejas, las hace un solo bloque.

La noche se ha encendido como una sorda hoguera
de llamas minerales y oscuras embestidas.
Y alrededor la sombra late como si fuera
las almas de los pozos y el vino difundidas.

Ya la sombra es el nido cerrado, incandescente,
la visible ceguera puesta sobre quien ama;
ya provoca el abrazo cerrado, ciegamente,
ya recoge en sus cuevas cuanto la luz derrama.

La sombra pide, exige seres que se entrelacen,
besos que la constelen de relámpagos largos,

CHILD OF LIGHT AND SHADOW

I. Child of Shadow

You are night, my wife: night at the peak
of its lunar, feminine power.
You are midnight: culminating shadow
where dreams culminate, where love culminates.

Forged by the day, my burning heart
bears the sun's huge imprint wherever you want
with a solar impulse, supreme light,
climax of mornings and nights.

I will fall across your body when night
spreads its greedy magnetic lust and power.
A febrile astral sadness seizes me,
inflames my bones with a chill.

The night air disturbs your breasts,
disturbs and capsizes bodies with a shock.
Like a storm of maddened beds
it eclipses couples, makes them a solid block.

The night is lit like a mute bonfire
of mineral flame and dark assaults.
All around, shadow throbs, as if it were
the diffusing souls of wells and wine.

Now shadow is the closed nest, incandescent,
visible blindness fixed on those in love;
now it provokes the closed embrace, blindly,
now it gathers, in its caves, whatever light spills.

Shadow begs for, it craves bodies that interlace,
kisses that form constellations of prolonged lightning,

bocas embravecidas, batidas, que atenacen,
arrullos que hagan música de sus mudos letargos.

Pide que nos echemos tú y yo sobre la manta,
tú y yo sobre la luna, tú y yo sobre la vida.
Pide que tú y yo ardamos fundiendo en la garganta,
con todo el firmamento, la tierra estremecida.

El hijo está en la sombra que acumula luceros,
amor, tuétano, luna, claras oscuridades.
Brota de sus perezas y de sus agujeros,
y de sus solitarias y apagadas ciudades.

El hijo está en la sombra: de la sombra ha surtido,
y a su origen infunden los astros una siembra,
un zumo lácteo, un flujo de cálido latido,
que ha de obligar sus huesos al sueño y a la hembra.

Moviendo está la sombra sus fuerzas siderales,
tendiendo está la sombra su constelada umbría,
volcando las parejas y haciéndolas nupciales.
Tú eres la noche, esposa. Yo soy el mediodía.

II. Hijo de la luz

Tú eres el alba, esposa: la principal penumbra,
recibes entornadas las horas de tu frente.
Decidido al fulgor, pero entornado, alumbra
tu cuerpo. Tus entrañas forjan el sol naciente.

Centro de claridades, la gran hora te espera
en el umbral de un fuego que el fuego mismo abrasa:
te espero yo, inclinado como el trigo a la era,
colocando en el centro de la luz nuestra casa.

La noche desprendida de los pozos oscuros,
se sumerge en los pozos donde ha echado raíces.

angry beaten mouths that rip the flesh,
lullabies that compose music from their mute lethargy.

It begs us both to throw ourselves onto the blanket,
throw ourselves over the moon and out into life.
It begs us both to burn, melting in our throats
the trembling earth with the whole firmament.

The child is in a shadow that collects morning stars,
love, marrow, moon, clear darknesses.
He springs from their leisure, and their empty places,
from their lonely, snuffed-out cities.

The child is in shadow: he has sprouted from shadow,
and stars begin their sowing at his origin,
a milky sap, a warm throbbing flow
that binds his bones to dreams and women.

That shadow is shifting its sidereal forces,
that shadow is spreading its starry shade,
capsizing couples and making them married.
You are night, my wife. I am the middle of the day.

II. Child of Light

You are dawn, my wife: the first penumbra,
your face lets in the half-closed hours.
Committed to brilliance, but half-closed, your body
produces light. Your entrails forge the rising sun.

Center of brightness, the great hour awaits you
on the threshold of a fire itself on fire:
I wait for you, bent like wheat to the threshing floor,
arranging our house in the center of the light.

The dark wells' generous night sinks
into wells where it has taken root.

Y tú te abres al parto luminoso, entre muros
que se rasgan contigo como pétreas matrices.

La gran hora del parto, la más rotunda hora:
estallan los relojes sintiendo tu alarido,
se abren todas las puertas del mundo, de la aurora,
y el sol nace en tu vientre donde encontró su nido.

El hijo fue primero sombra y ropa cosida
por tu corazón hondo desde tus hondas manos.
Con sombras y con ropas anticipó su vida,
con sombras y con ropas de gérmenes humanos.

Las sombras y las ropas sin población, desiertas,
se han poblado de un niño sonoro, un movimiento,
que en nuestra casa pone de par en par las puertas,
y ocupa en ella a gritos el luminoso asiento.

¡Ay, la vida: qué hermoso penar tan moribundo!
Sombras y ropas trajo la del hijo que nombras.
Sombras y ropas llevan los hombres por el mundo.
Y todos dejan siempre sombras: ropas y sombras.

Hijo del alba eres, hijo del mediodía.
Y ha de quedar de ti luces en todo impuestas,
mientras tu madre y yo vamos a la agonía,
dormidos y despiertos con el amor a cuestas.

Hablo y el corazón me sale en el aliento
Si no hablara lo mucho que quiero me ahogaría.
Con espliego y resinas perfumo tu aposento.
Tú eres el alba, esposa Yo soy el mediodía.

III. *Hijo de la luz y de la sombra*

Tejidos en el alba, grabados, dos panales
no pueden detener la miel en los pezones.

And you open yourself to radiant childbirth,
between walls, breached, as you are, like stone matrices.

Childbirth's great hour, the roundest hour:
clocks burst, hearing you howl,
all the world's doors, and dawn's, fly open,
and the sun is born in your womb, its nest.

At first the child was shadow and cloth, sewn
by your deep hands from your heart's depths.
With shadows and cloth he anticipated his life,
with the shadows and clothing of human seed.

Shadows and clothes, deserted, with nobody in them,
have been filled with a squalling boy, a movement
that throws the doors of our house wide open
and occupies, shouting, a luminous spot.

Ay, life! What beautiful grief so near death!
Shadows and cloth gave the life of the child you name.
Men wear shadows and cloth all over the world.
And they always leave shadows behind: cloth and shadow.

You are dawn's child, noon's child.
And in our care, asleep, awake, with love,
you will leave light imposed on everything
while your mother and I move toward agony.

I speak, and my heart escapes in my breath.
If I could not say how full of love I am, I would drown.
I perfume your room with lavender and resin.
You are dawn, my wife. I am the middle of the day.

III. *Child of Light and Shadow*

Woven in the dawn, engraved, two honeycombs
can't hold back the honey from their nipples.

Tus pechos en el alba: maternos manantiales,
luchan y se atropellan con blancas efusiones.

Se han desbordado, esposa, lunarmente tus venas,
hasta inundar la casa que tu sabor rezuma.
Y es como sí brotaras de un pueblo de colmenas,
tú toda una colmena de leche con espuma.

Es como si tu sangre fuera dulzura toda,
laboriosas abejas filtradas por tus poros.
Oigo un clamor de leche, de inundación, de boda
junto a ti, recorrida por caudales sonoros.

Caudalosa mujer: en tu vientre me entierro.
Tu caudaloso vientre será mi sepultura.
Si quemaran mis huesos con la llama del hierro,
verían qué grabada llevo allí tu figura.

Para siempre fundidos en el hijo quedamos:
fundidos como anhelan nuestras ansias voraces:
en un ramo de tiempo, de sangre, los dos ramos,
en un haz de caricias, de pelo, los dos haces.

Los muertos, con un fuego congelado que abrasa,
laten junto a los vivos de una manera terca.
Viene a ocupar el hijo los campos y la casa
que tú y yo abandonamos quedándonos muy cerca.

Haremos de este hijo generador sustento,
y hará de nuestra carne materia decisiva:
donde sienten su alma las manos y el aliento
las hélices circulen, la agricultura viva

El hará que esta vida no caiga derribada,
pedazo desprendido de nuestros dos pedazos,
que de nuestras dos bocas hará una sola espada
y dos brazos eternos de nuestros cuatro brazos.

Your breasts in the dawn: maternal springs
that struggle, that rush with white effusions.

Your veins have overflowed, my wife, like the moon,
till they flood the house your savour fills.
And it is as if you oozed from a village of beehives,
you, a whole beehive of foaming milk.

As if your blood were all sweetness,
busy bees filtering through your pores.
I hear a commotion of milk, of flooding, of the marriage
beside you, overrun with resounding abundance.

Abundant woman: I bury myself in your womb.
Your plentiful womb will be my grave.
If my bones burned with iron flame
they would see that I carry your image engraved there.

We are forged together forever in our child:
a fusion our greedy desires long for—
our two branches in one bough of time, and blood;
our two sheaves in one bundle of caresses, and hair.

The dead, burning with frozen fire,
throb stubbornly inside the living:
a child is coming to take up the fields and house
that you and I are leaving, though we stay close by.

We will make this child a generative support,
and he will make final matter of our flesh:
where his hands and breath set down his soul,
propellers will whirl, crops will prosper.

Loose fragment of our own two fragments,
he will make sure that this life is not discarded;
of our two mouths he will make one sword,
and of our four arms, two eternal arms.

No te quiero a ti sola: te quiero en tu ascendencia
y en cuanto de tu vientre descenderá mañana.
Porque la especie humana me han dado por herencia
la familia del hijo será la especie humana.

Con el amor a cuestas, dormidos y despiertos,
seguiremos besándonos en el hijo profundo.
Besándonos tú y yo se besan nuestros muertos,
se besan los primeros pobladores del mundo.

I do not love you alone: I love you in your ancestors,
and in all who will descend from your womb tomorrow.
Because the human race has been given as my heritage
the child's family will be the human race.

With love in our care, asleep and awake,
we will always be kissing in our deep child.
Kissing each other, our dead are kissing,
the first inhabitants of the world are kissing.

DON SHARE

EXCERPTO DE LA LLUVIA

Han enmudecido el campo, presintiendo la lluvia.
Reaparece en la tierra su primer abandono.
La alegriá del cielo se desconsuela a veces,
sobre un pastor sediento.

Cuando la lluvia llama se remueven los muertos.
La tierra se hace un hoyo removido, oloroso.
Los árboles exhalan su último olor profundo
dispuestos a morirse.

Bajo la lluvia adquiere la voz de los relojes
la gran edad, la anguista de la postrera hora.
Señalan las heridas visibles y las otras
que sangran hacia adentro.

Todo se hace entrañable, reconcentrado, íntimo.
Como bajo el subsuelo, bajo el signo lluvioso
todo, todo parece desear ahora
la paz definitiva.

Llueve como un sangre transparente, hechizada.
Me siento traspasado por la humedad del suelo
que habrá de sujetarme para siempre a la sombra,
para siempre a la lluvia.

El cielo se desangra pausadamente herido.
El verde intensifica la penumbra en las hojas.
Los troncos y los muertos se oscurecen aún más
por la pasión del agua.

62

FROM *THE RAIN*

Still fields. A feeling of rain.
The earth wild and primitive as it was once before.
Sometimes the joyful sky gets tired of it all
above a thirsty shepherd.

When the rain calls, the dead turn uneasily.
The earth becomes a hole, stirred up, fragrant.
Trees that are ready for death give off
their last deep fragrance.

In the rain the voice of the clocks takes on
the immense age, the agony of the last hour.
They make us aware of the visible wounds, and those
    others
that bleed internally.

Everything grows deep, concentrated, personal.
Things beneath the rain-sign, as if already deep in the
    ground,
all seem to want
the final peace.

The rain is like mysterious drops of blood that you can
    see through.
I feel the dampness of the ground go through me,
it would like to keep me in the dark forever,
in the rain forever.

The sky is losing blood slowly out of wounds.
The green deepens the shadows under leaves.
The passion of the water makes the trunks and the bodies
lean more and more in darkness.

TIMOTHY BALAND

Beso soy, sombra con sombra.
Beso, dolor con dolor,
por haberme enamorado,
corazón sin corazón,
de las cosas, del aliento
sin sombra de la creación.
Sed con agua en la distancia,
pero sed alrededor.

Corazón en una copa
donde me lo bebo yo
y no se lo bebe nadie,
nadie sabe su sabor.
Odio, vida: ¡cuánto odio
sólo por amor!

No es posible acariciarte
con las manos que me dio
el fuego de más deseo
el ansia de más ardor.
Varias alas, varios vuelos
abaten en ellas hoy
hierros que cercan las venas
y las muerden con rencor.
Por amor, vida, abatido,
pájaro sin remisión.
Sólo por amor odiado,
sólo por amor.

Amor, tu bóveda arriba
y yo abajo siempre amor,
sin otra luz que estas ansias,
sin otra iluminación.
Mírame aquí encadenado,
escupido, sin calor,

BEFORE HATRED

I am a kiss, a shadow with shadow.
A kiss, pain with pain,
for having fallen in love,
heartless heart,
of things, of breath
without the shadow of creation.
Thirsting, with water in the distance,
but thirst everywhere.

My heart in a cup
where I drink it down
and no one else drinks it.
No one knows its taste.
Hatred, life: so much hate,
because of love!

It is not possible to caress you
with hands that have kindled
the greatest desire,
the most heated longing.
Many wings, much flight
is pulled down today by
chains that cuff the veins
and bite them with rancor.
For love, life. Shot down
unforgiven bird.
Hated, because of love,
because of love.

Love, you the vault above,
and I, the love, always below,
with no light other than these yearnings,
no other illumination.
Look at me chained down here,
spit upon, with no warmth

a los pies de la tiniebla
más súbita, más feroz,
comiendo pan y cuchillo
como buen trabajador
y a veces cuchillo sólo,
sólo por amor.

Todo lo que significa
golondrinas, ascensión,
claridad, anchura, aire,
decidido espacio, sol,
horizonte aleteante,
sepultado en un rincón.
Esperanza, mar, desierto,
sangre, monte rodador:
libertades de mi alma
clamorosas de pasión,
desfilando por mi cuerpo,
donde no se quedan, no,
pero donde se despliegan,
sólo por amor.

Porque dentro de la triste
guirnalda del eslabón,
de sabor a carcelero
constante, y a paredón,
y a precipicio en acecho,
alto, alegre, libre soy.
Alto, alegre, libre, libre,
sólo por amor.

No, no hay cárcel para el hombre.
No podrán atarme, no.
Este mundo de cadenas
me es pequeño y exterior.
¿Quién encierra una sonrisa?
¿Quién amuralla una voz?
A lo lejos, más sola
que la muerte, la una y yo.

at the mercy of the fiercest,
most sudden darkness,
taking bread and knife
like a good worker.
And sometimes the knife,
because of love.

All that it signifies:
swallows, ascent,
clarity, breadth, air,
definite space, sun,
a fluttering horizon—
buried in a corner.
Hope, sea, desert,
blood, rolling mountains:
liberties my soul takes
crying out for passion,
filing past my body
without pausing, no,
spreading out,
because of love.

Because caught here in the sad
garland of chains,
that smacks of the jailer,
constant, and the executioner's wall,
at the edge of an abyss in ambush,
I am uplifted, happy, free.
Uplifted, happy, free, free,
because of love.

No, there is no jail for man.
They can't shackle me, no.
This world of chains
is small and foreign to me.
Who locks up a smile?
Who walls in a voice?
There you are in the distance, more alone
than death, you and I.

A lo lejos tú, sintiendo
en tus brazos mi prisión,
en tus brazos donde late
la libertad de los dos.
Libre soy. Siénteme libre.
Sólo por amor.

You are far away, feeling
my prison in your arms,
in your arms, where freedom
beats like a heart for the two of us.
I am free. Feel me free.
Because of love.

TED GENOWAYS

LA BOCA

Boca que arrastra mi boca.
Boca que me has arrastrado:
boca que vienes de lejos
a iluminarme de rayos.

Alba que das a mis noches
un resplandor rojo y blanco.
Boca poblada de bocas:
pájaro lleno de pájaros.
Canción que vuelve las alas
hacia arriba y hacia abajo.
Muerte reducida a besos,
a sed de morir despacio,
das a la grama sangrante
dos tremendos aletazos.
El labio de arriba el cielo
y la tierra el otro labio.

Beso que rueda en la sombra:
beso que viene rodando
desde el primer cementerio
hasta los últimos astros.
Astro que tiene tu boca
enmudecido y cerrado,
hasta que un roce celeste
hace que vibren sus párpados.

Beso que va a un porvenir
de muchachas y muchachos,
que no dejarán desiertos
ni las calles ni los campos.

¡Cuánta boca ya enterrada,
sin boca, desenterramos!

MOUTH

Mouth that pulls at my mouth.
Mouth that has pulled me along;
mouth that comes from afar
with beams to illuminate me.

Dawn that fires my nights
a red and white radiance.
Mouth crowded with mouths:
bird full of birds.
Song winging its way
upward and down.
Death that subsides into kisses,
into a thirst to die slowly,
you give the blood-stained grass
two wingbeats that gleam.
The upper lip, sky,
the lower lip, earth.

Kiss moving through darkness:
kiss that comes rolling
out of the first graveyard
toward the outermost stars.
Star that has silenced
and stopped your mouth
until a celestial dew
flutters your eyelids.

Kiss moving toward the boys
and girls of tomorrow
who won't let the streets
or the fields lie empty.

Mouths, however many now buried,
mouthless—we are digging up!

Bebo en tu boca por ellos,
brindo en tu boca por tantos
que cayeron sobre el vino
de los amorosos vasos.
Hoy son recuerdos, recuerdos,
besos distantes y amargos.

Hundo en tu boca mi vida,
oigo rumores de espacios,
y el infinito parece
que sobre mí se ha volcado.

He de volver a besarte,
he de volver. Hundo, caigo
mientras descienden los siglos
hacia los hondos barrancos
como una febril nevada
de besos y enamorados.

Boca que desenterraste
el amanecer más claro
con tu lengua. Tres palabras,
tres fuegos has heredado:
Vida, Muerte, Amor. Ahi quedan
escritos sobre tus labios.

I drink for them from your mouth,
with your mouth I toast all those
who'd imbibe the wine
in their loving glasses.
They're memories now, only memories'
kisses turned sour and gone.

I sink my life in your mouth.
I hear the booming of space,
and infinity seems
to have poured itself over me.

I shall return to kiss you,
I have to return, and falling
sink with the centuries
descending into the deep ravines
like a feverish snowfall
of lovers' kisses.

Mouth that with your tongue
drew out of the earth
the brightest dawn. Three words,
three fires you have inherited:
life, death, love. There they abide,
inscribed on your lips.

EDWIN HONIG

ASCENSIÓN DE LA ESCOBA

Coronada la escoba de laurel, mirto, rosa,
Es el héroe entre aquellos que afrontan la basura.
Para librar del polvo sin vuelo cada cosa
Bajó, porque era palma y azul, desde la altura.

Su ardor de espada joven y alegre no reposa.
Delgada de ansiedad, pureza, sol, bravura,
Azucena que barre sobre la misma fosa,
Es cada vez más alta, más cálida, más pura.

¡Nunca! La escoba nunca será crucificada,
porque la juventud propaga su esqueleto
que es una sola flauta, muda, pero sonora.

Es una sola lengua sublime y acordada.
Y ante su aliento raudo se ausenta el polvo quieto,
Y asciende una palmera, columna hacia la aurora.

Cárcel de Torrijos, Septiembre de 1939

ASCENSION OF THE BROOM

The broom, costumed in myrtle, rose, and bay,
the hero among us who face the trash,
frees everything from dust that cannot fly,
since it was palm tree blue and dropped to earth.

Fiery and young, a constant cheerful sword,
slender with worry, pure, courageous, sun,
the lily sweeps the floor—our grave and ward—
moves higher, hotter, purer than a gun.

Never! The broom will not be crucified,
our youth is propagating a long bone,
a lonely flute of mountain notes, though mute,

a lonely tongue, sublime, perfect in tone.
Before its breath the quiet dust has died,
and a palm tree, a column climbs toward dawn.

Torrijos Prison, September 1939

WILLIS BARNSTONE

DESPUÉS DEL AMOR

No pudimos ser. La tierra
no pudo tanto. No somos
cuanto se propuso el sol
en un anhelo remoto.
Un pie se acerca a lo claro,
en lo oscuro insiste el otro.
Porque el amor no es perpetuo
en nadie, ni en mí tampoco.
El odio aguarda un instante
dentro del carbón más hondo.
Rojo es el odio y nutrido.
El amor, pálido y solo.
Cansado de odiar, te amo.
Cansado de amar, te odio.

Llueve tiempo, llueve tiempo.
Y un día triste entre todos,
triste por toda la tierra,
triste desde mí hasta el lobo,
dormimos y despertamos
con un tigre entre los ojos.

Piedras, hombres como piedras,
duros y plenos de encono,
chocan en el aire, donde
chocan las piedras de pronto.
Soledades que hoy rechazan
y ayer juntaban sus rostros.
Soledades que en el beso
guardan el rugido sordo.
Soledades, para siempre.
Soledades sin apoyo.

Cuerpos como un mar voraz
entrechocando, furioso.

AFTER LOVE

We could not be. The earth
could not be enough. We are not
what the sun intended
in its distant yearning.
One foot approaches the light.
The other insists on darkness.
Because love doesn't last forever
in anyone, not even me.
Hatred waits for its moment
in the coal's deepest core.
Hatred is red and well-fed.
Love is pale and solitary.
Tired of hating, I love you.
Tired of loving, I hate you.

It is raining time, drizzling time.
And one sad day,
sad for the whole earth,
sad from me to the wolf,
we sleep and wake up
with a tiger in our eyes.

Stones, men like stones,
hard and full of hostility,
collide in the air, where
rocks suddenly collide.
Solitudes, which today repel,
and yesterday drew together.
Solitudes, which in a kiss
conceal a deafening roar.
Solitudes, forever.
Solitudes without comfort.

Bodies like a voracious sea,
thrashing, furious.

Solitariamente atados
por el amor, por el odio.
Por las venas surgen hombres,
cruzan las ciudades, torvos.

En el corazón arraiga
solitariamente todo.
Huellas sin compaña quedan
como en el agua, en el fondo.

Sólo una voz, a lo lejos,
siempre a lo lejos la oigo,
acompaña y hace ir
igual que el cuello a los hombros.

Sólo una voz me arrebata
este armazón espinoso
de vello retrocedido
y erizado que me pongo.

Los secos vientos no pueden
secar los mares jugosos.
Y el corazón permanece
fresco en su cárcel de agosto,
porque esa voz es el arma
mas tierna de los arroyos:

«Miguel: me acuerdo de ti
después del sol y del polvo,
antes de la misma luna,
tumba de un sueño amoroso.»

Amor: aleja mi ser
de sus primeros escombros,
y edificándome, dicta
una verdad como un soplo.
Después del amor, la tierra.
Después de la tierra, todo.

Lonely, tied together
in isolation by hate,
men surge in the veins,
and cross the cities grimly.

In the heart everything
takes root in isolation.
Lonely footsteps are left behind
as if under water, on the bottom.

Only one voice, so distant,
I always hear it distantly,
it accompanies me, forces me on—
like a neck to the shoulders.

Only one voice snatches from me
from this thorny scaffolding
of receding and bristling hair,
I clothe myself in.

The dry winds cannot
dry out the succulent oceans.
And the heart goes on
fresh in its harvest-time jail
because that voice is the tide's
most tender weapon:

"Miguel, I remember you
after the sun and the dust,
before the moon itself,
tomb of a loving dream."

Love: separate my existence
from its first ruins,
and constructing me, pronounce
one truth like a gust of wind.
After love, the earth.
After the earth, everything.

TED GENOWAYS

[*EL MUNDO ES COMO APARECE*]

El mundo es como aparece
ante mis cinco sentidos,
y ante los tuyos que son
las orillas de los míos.
El mundo de los demás
no es el nuestro: no es el mismo.
Lecho de agua que soy,
tú, los dos, somos el río
donde cuando más profundo
se ve más despacio y límpido.
Imágenes de la vida:
a la vez que recibimos,
nos reciben entregadas
más unidamente a un ritmo.
Pero las cosas se forman
con nuestros propios delirios.
El aire tiene el tamaño
del corazón que respiro
y el sol es como la luz
con que yo le desafío.
Ciegos para los demás,
oscuros, siempre remisos,
miramos siempre hacia adentro,
vemos desde lo más íntimo.
Trabajo y amor me cuesta
conmigo así, ver contigo;
aparecer, como el agua
con la arena, siempre unidos.
Nadie me verá del todo
ni es nadie como lo miro.
Somos algo más que vemos,
algo menos que inquirimos.
Algún suceso de todos
pasa desapercibido.

[THE WORLD IS AS IT APPEARS]

The world is as it appears
before my five senses,
and before yours, which are
the borders of my own.
The others' world
is not ours: not the same.
You are the body of water
that I am—we, together,
are the river
which as it grows deeper
is seen to run slower, clearer.
Images of life—
as soon as we receive them,
they receive us, delivered
jointly, in one rhythm.
But things form themselves
in our own delirium.
The air has the hugeness
of the heart I breathe,
and the sun is like the light
with which I challenge it.
Blind to the others,
dark, always remiss,
we always look inside,
we see from the most intimate places.
It takes work and love
to see these things with you;
to appear, like water
with sand, always one.
No one will see me completely.
Nor is anyone the way I see him.
We are something more than we see,
something less than we look into.
Some parts of the whole
pass unnoticed.

Nadie nos ha visto. A nadie
ciegos de ver, hemos visto.

No one has seen us. We have seen
no one, blind as we are from seeing.

DON SHARE

GUERRA

Todas las madres del mundo
ocultan el vientre, tiemblan,
y quisieran retirarse
a virginidades ciegas,
al origen solitario
y el pasado sin herencia.

Pálida, sobrecogida
la virginidad se queda.
El mar gime sed y gime
sed de ser agua la tierra.
Alarga la llama el odio
y el clamor cierra las puertas.

Voces como lanzas vibran,
voces como bayonetas.
Bocas como puños vienen,
puños como cascos llegan.
Pechos como muros roncos,
piernas como patas recias.

El corazón se revuelve,
se atorbellina, revienta.
Arroja contra los ojos
súbitas espumas negras.

La sangre enarbola el cuerpo,
precipita la cabeza
y busca un cuerpo, una herida
por donde lanzarse afuera.
La sangre recorre el mundo
enjaulada, insatisfecha.
Las flores se desvanecen
devoradas por la hierba.
Ansias de matar invaden
el fondo de la azucena.

WAR

All the mothers in the world
hide their wombs, tremble,
and wish they could turn back
into blind virginities,
into that solitary beginning,
the past, with nothing before it.

Virginity is left
pale, frightened.
The sea howls thirst and the earth
howls to be water.
Hatred flames out,
and the screaming slams doors.

Voices shake like lances,
voices like bayonets.
Mouths step forward like fists,
fists arrive like hooves.
Breasts like hoarse walls,
legs like sinewy paws.

The heart quickens,
storms, blows up.
It throws sudden black spume
into the eye.

Blood thrashes about in the body,
flings the head off,
and searches for another body, a wound
to leap through, outside.
Blood parades through the world
caged, baffled.
Flowers wither,
devoured by the grass.
A lust for murder possesses
the secret places of the lily.

Acoplarse con metales
todos los cuerpos anhelan:
desposarse, poseerse
de una terrible manera.

Desaparecer: el ansia
general, naciente, reina.
Un fantasma de estandartes,
una bandera quimérica,
un mito de patrias: una
grave ficción de fronteras.

Músicas exasperadas,
duras como botas, huellan
la faz de las esperanzas
y de las entrañas tiernas.
Crepita el alma, la ira.
El llanto relampaguea.
¿Para qué quiero la luz
si tropiezo con tinieblas?

Pasiones como clarines,
coplas, trompas que aconsejan
devorarse ser a ser,
destruirse piedra a piedra.
Relinchos. Retumbos. Truenos.
Salivazos. Besos. Ruedas.
Espuelas. Espadas locas
abren una herida inmensa.
Después, el silencio, mudo
de algodón, blanco de vendas,
cárdeno de cirugía,
mutilado de tristeza.
El silencio. Y el laurel
en un rincón de osamentas.
Y un tambor enamorado,
como un vientre tenso, suena
detrás del innumberable
muerto que jamás se aleja.

Every living body longs to be joined
to a piece of cold metal:
to be married and possessed horribly.

To disappear: a vast anxiety
spreading, rules everything.
A ghostly procession of banners,
a fantastic flag,
a myth of nations: a
grave fiction of frontiers.

Outraged musics,
tough as boots, scar
the face of every hope
and the tender core.
The soul rages, fury.
Tears burst like lightning.
What do I want with light,
if I stumble into darkness?

Passions like horns,
songs, trumpets that urge
the living to eat the living,
to tear themselves down stone by stone.
Whinnies. Reverberations. Thunder.
Slaverings. Kisses. Wheels.
Spurs. Crazy swords
tear open a huge wound.
Then silence, mute
as cotton, white as bandages,
scarlet as surgery,
mutilated as sadness.
Silence. And laurel
in a corner among bones.
And a hysterical drum,
a tense womb, beats
behind the innumerable
dead man who never gets past.

JAMES WRIGHT

NANAS DE LA CEBOLLA

La cebolla es escarcha
cerrada y pobre:
escarcha de tus días
y de mis noches.
Hambre y cebolla:
hielo negro y escarcha
grande y redonda.

En la cuna del hambre
mi niño estaba.
Con sangre de cebolla
se amamantaba.
Pero tu sangre,
escarchada de azúcar,
cebolla y hambre.

Una mujer morena,
resuelta en luna,
se derrama hilo a hilo
sobre la cuna.
Ríete, niño,
que te tragas la luna
cuando es preciso.

Alondra de mi casa,
ríete mucho.
Es tu risa en los ojos
la luz del mundo.
Ríete tanto
que en el alma, al oírte,
bata el espacio.

Tu risa me hace libre,
me pone alas.
Soledades me quita,

LULLABIES OF THE ONION

The onion is frost
shut in and poor.
Frost of your days
and of my nights.
Hunger and onion,
black ice and frost
large and round.

My little boy was
in hunger's cradle.
He suckled on
onion blood.
But your blood is
frosted with sugar,
onion and hunger.

A dark woman dissolved
into moonlight
spills, thread by thread,
over the cradle.
Laugh, child,
you can drink moonlight
if you have to.

Lark of my house,
laugh freely.
Your laughter in your eyes
is the world's light.
Laugh so much
that hearing you, my soul
will beat through space.

Your laughter frees me,
gives me wings.
It banishes loneliness,

cárcel me arranca.
Boca que vuela,
corazón que en tus labios
relampaguea.

Es tu risa la espada
más victoriosa.
Vencedor de las flores
y las alondras.
Rival del sol,
porvenir de mis huesos
y de mi amor.

La carne aleteante,
súbito el párpado,
el niño como nunca
coloreado.
¡Cuánto jilguero
se remonta, aletea,
desde tu cuerpo!

Desperté de ser niño.
Nunca despiertes.
Triste llevo la boca.
Ríete siempre.
Siempre en la cuna,
defendiendo la risa
pluma por pluma.

Ser de vuelo tan alto,
tan extendido,
que tu carne es el cielo
recién nacido.
¡Si yo pudiera
remontarme al origen
de tu carrera!

Al octavo mes ríes
con cinco azahares.

tears down these walls.
Mouth that flies,
heart that flashes
on your lips.

Your laughter is
the supreme sword,
conqueror of flowers
and larks.
Rival of the sun.
Future of my bones
and of my love.

The flesh flutters,
as sudden as an eyelid,
life, as never before,
takes on new color.
How many linnets,
wings beating, take off
from your body!

I woke from childhood:
don't you ever.
I wear my mouth sadly:
always laugh.
Stay always in your cradle
defending laughter
feather by feather.

You are a flight
so high, so wide,
that your flesh is heaven
just born.
If only I could climb
to the origin
of your flight!

In the eight months you laugh
with five orange blossoms.

Con cinco diminutas
ferocidades.
Con cinco dientes
como cinco jazmines
adolescentes.

Frontera de los besos
serán mañana,
cuando en la dentadura
sientas un arma.
Sientas un fuego
correr dientes abajo
buscando el centro.

Vuela niño en la doble
luna del pecho.
Él, triste de cebolla.
Tú, satisfecho.
No te derrumbes.
No sepas lo que pasa
ni lo que ocurre.

With five little
ferocities,
with five teeth
like five young
jasmine buds.

They will be the frontier
of kisses tomorrow
when you feel a gun
in your mouth.
When you feel a burning
past the teeth
searching for the center.

Fly, child, on the double moon
of her breast;
it is saddened by onion,
you are satisfied.
Never let go.
Don't ever know what's coming,
what goes on.

PHILIP LEVINE

EL ÚLTIMO RINCÓN

El último y el primero:
rincón para el sol más grande,
sepultura de esta vida
donde tus ojos no caben.

Allí quisiera tenderme
para desenamorarme.

Por el olivo lo quiero,
lo percibo por la calle,
se sume por los rincones
donde se sumen los árboles.

Se ahonda y hace más honda
la intensidad de mi sangre.

Los olivos moribundos
florecen en todo el aire
y los muchachos se quedan
cercanos y agonizantes.

Carne de mi movimiento,
huesos de ritmos mortales:
me muero por respirar
sobre vuestros ademanes.

Corazón que entre dos piedras
ansiosas de machacarte,
de tanto querer te ahogas
como un mar entre dos mares.

De tanto querer me ahogo,
y no es posible ahogarme.

Beso que viene rodando
desde el principio del mundo

THE LAST CORNER

The last and the first:
corner for the greatest sun,
tomb of this life
with no room for your eyes.

I would like to stretch out there
to fall out of love.

I want it near the olive tree,
I sense it in the streets,
it sinks back in corners
where the trees sink.

It burrows into and deepens
the intensity of my blood.

The dying olive trees
bloom in all the air
and the boys remain
near and dying.

Flesh of my movement,
blood of my mortal rhythms:
I am dying from breathing
over everything you do.

Heart, between two stones
anxious to crush you,
you drown in so much love
like a sea between two seas.

I drown in so much love,
yet I can't drown myself.

Kiss that comes rolling
from the beginning of the world

a mi boca por tus labios.
Beso que va al porvenir,
boca como un doble astro
que entre los astros palpita
por tantos besos parados,
por tantos bocas cerradas
sin un beso solitario.

¿Qué hice para que pusieran
a mi vida tanta cárcel?

Tu pelo donde lo negro
ha sufrido las edades
de la negrura más firme,
y la más emocionante:
tu secular pelo negro
recorro hasta remontarme
a la negrura primera
de tus ojos y tus padres,
al rincón del pelo denso
donde relampagueaste.

Como un rincón solitario
allí el hombre brota y arde.

Ay, él rincón de tu vientre;
el callejón de tu carne:
el callejón sin salida
donde agonicé una tarde.

La pólvora y el amor
marchan sobre las ciudades
deslumbrando, removiendo
la población de la sangre.

El naranjo sabe a vida
y el olivo a tiempo sabe.
Y entre el clamor de los dos
mis pasiones se debaten.

to my mouth by your lips.
Kiss that goes to the future,
mouth like a double star
that beats between the stars
because of so many stopped kisses,
because of so many mouths closed
without a solitary kiss.

What did I do to make them put
so much jail in my life?

Your black hair
has suffered through ages
of the most profound
and most moving blackness:
I traverse that ageless black hair
until I reach
the first blackness
of your eyes and your parents:
to the corner of thick hair
where you flashed like lightning.

Like a solitary corner,
man appears and burns there.

Yes, the corner of your womb,
the alley-way of your body,
the blind alley
of my death-throes one afternoon.

Gunpowder and love
march through the cities,
dazzling, stirring
the population of the blood.

The orange tree tastes of life
and the olive tree tastes of time
and between the clamoring two
my passions debate.

El último y el primero:
rincón donde algún cadáver
siente el arrullo del mundo
de los amorosos cauces.

Siesta que ha entenebrecido
el sol de las humedades.

Allí quisiera tenderme
para desenamorarme.

Después del amor, la tierra.
Después de la tierra, nadie.

The last and the first:
corner where some corpse
sings the world to sleep
on its riverbed of love.

Sleep that has darkened
the sun of dank places.

There I would like to stretch out
to fall out of love.

After love, the earth.
After the earth, no one.

TED GENOWAYS

CANTAR

Es la casa un palomar
y la cama un jazminero.
Las puertas de par en par
y en el fondo el mundo entero.

El hijo, tu corazón
madre que se ha engrandecido.
Dentro de la habitación
todo lo que ha florecido.

El hijo te hace un jardín,
y tú has hecho al hijo, esposa,
la habitación del jazmin,
el palomar de la rosa.

Alrededor de tu piel
ato y desato la mía.
Un mediodía de miel
rezumas: un mediodía.

¿Quién en esta casa entró
y la apartó del desierto?
Para que me acuerde yo
alguien que soy yo y ha muerto.

Viene la luz más redonda
a los almendros más blancos.
La vida, la luz se ahonda
entre muertos y barrancos.

Venturoso es el futuro,
como aquellos horizontes
de pórfido y mármol puro
donde respiran los montes.

TO SING

The house is a dovecote
and the bed is a bed of jasmines.
The door is wide open
to the whole world.

The child: your motherly heart
grown large.
In these rooms:
everything that has blossomed.

The child makes you into a garden,
and you, my wife, make the child into
a room full of jasmine,
a dovecote of rose.

Around your skin
I bind and unbind my own.
You exude a noontime
of honey: a noon.

Who entered this house
and left it deserted?
I remember:
I am somebody, and he has died.

Roundest light comes
to the whitest almond trees.
Life, and light digs deeply down
among the dead men and the gullies.

The future is prosperous,
like those horizons
of pure porphyry and marble
where mountains breathe.

Arde la casa encendida
de besos y sombra amante.
No puede pasar la vida
más honda y emocionante.

Desbordadamente sorda
la leche alumbra tus huesos.
Y la casa se desborda
con ella, el hijo y los besos.

Tú, tu vientre caudaloso,
el hijo y el palomar.
Esposa, sobre tu esposo
suenan los pasos del mar.

The house, kindled
by kissing and love's shadow, burns.
Life can't go on
more deeply, more charged than this.

Mute and overflowing, milk
illuminates your bones.
And the house, with child and kisses,
is flooded with it.

You, your abundant womb,
the child and the dove.
My wife, over your husband
the sea's passage resounds.

DON SHARE

CASIDA DEL SEDIENTO

Arena del desierto
Soy: desierto de sed.
Oasis es tu boca
Donde no he de beber.

Boca: oasis abierto
A todas las arenas del desierto.

Húmedo punto en medio
De un mundo abrasador,
El de tu cuerpo, el tuyo,
Que nunca es de los dos.

Cuerpo: pozo cerrado
A quien la sed y el sol han calcinado.

Ocaña, mayo de 1941

LAMENT OF THE THIRSTING MAN

> I am sand of the desert:
> desert of thirst.
> Your mouth is an oasis
> where I shall not drink.
>
> Mouth: oasis open
> to all the sands of the desert.
>
> Watering-hole in the middle
> of a burning world,
> your body, yours
> but never ours.
>
> Body: a sealed well,
> mortared by the sun and thirst.

Ocaña, May 1941

TED GENOWAYS

[SONREÍR CON LA ALEGRE TRISTEZA DEL OLIVO]

Sonreír con la alegre tristeza del olivo.
Esperar. No cansarse de esperar la alegría.
Sonriamos. Doremos la luz de cada día
en esta alegre y triste vanidad del ser vivo.

Me siento cada día más libre y más cautivo
en toda esta sonrisa tan clara y tan sombría.
Cruzan las tempestades sobre tu boca fría
como sobre la míacutea que aún es un soplo estivo.

Una sonrisa se alza sobre el abismo: crece
como un abismo trémulo, pero valiente en alas.
Una sonrisa eleva calientemente el vuelo.

Diurna, firme, arriba, no baja, no anochece.
Todo lo desafías, amor: todo lo escalas.
Con sonrisa te fuiste de la tierra y del cielo.

[TO SMILE WITH THE CHEERFUL GRIEF OF THE OLIVE TREE]

To smile with the cheerful grief of the olive tree,
to hope for happiness, hope to survive
smiling, plating each day with gold, and be
this glad, sad vanity of being alive.

And every day I feel lighter and caught
up in that smile of brilliance and black shade.
Stormwinds punish your mouth freezing and taut
while mine is struck by summer winds that strayed

into my cell. A smile soars the abyss
and grows like a shocked pit—yet flapping wings.
A smile climbs hotly over caves, in flight,

diurnal, firm. It will not drop or miss
or darken. Love, you brave and climb all things,
and smiling fled the earth, the sky, the light.

WILLIS BARNSTONE

Riéndose, burlándose con claridad del día,
se hundió en la noche el niño que quise ser dos veces.
No quiso más la luz. ¿Para qué? No saldría
más de aquellos silencios, de aquellas lobregueces.

Quise ser . . . ¿Para qué? . . . Quise llegar gozoso
al centro de la esfera de todo lo que existe.
Quise llevar la risa como lo más hermoso.
He muerto sonriendo serenamente triste.

Niño dos veces niño: tres veces venidero.
Vuelve a rodar por ese mundo opaco del vientre.
Atrás, amor. Atrás, niño, porque no quiero
salir donde la luz su gran tristeza encuentre.

Regreso al aire plástico que alentó mi inconsciencia.
Vuelvo a rodar, consciente del sueño que me cubre.
En una sensitiva sombra de transparencia,
en un espacio íntimo rodar de octubre a octubre.

Vientre: carne central de todo cuanto existe.
Bóveda eternamente si azul, si roja, oscura.
Noche final, en cuya profundidad se siente
la voz de las raíces, el soplo de la altura.

Bajo tu piel avanzo, y es sangre la distancia.
Mi cuerpo en una densa constelación gravita.
El universo agolpa su errante resonancia
allí, donde la historia del hombre ha sido escrita.

Mirar y ver en torno la soledad, el monte,
el mar, por la ventana de un corazón entero
que ayer se acongojaba de no ser horizonte
abierto a un mundo menos mudable y pasajero.

CHILD OF THE NIGHT

Laughing, playing, bright like day,
the child I twice wanted to be fell into night.
He didn't want light any more. What for? He would never
emerge from those silences again, from that gloom.

I wanted to be . . . What for? I want to reach, joyously,
the center of the sphere of everything there is.
I wanted to take a smile, the most beautiful thing, with me.
I died smiling, serenely sad.

Child twice a child: three times coming.
Go back, churning through the womb's opaque world.
Back, love. Back, child, because I don't want
to come out where light finds its great sadness.

I return to the plastic air that inspired my
       unconsciousness.
I churn again, conscious of the sleep that blankets me.
In a sensitive shadow of transparency,
an intimate space churning from October to October.

Womb: core flesh of everything there is.
Eternal cave, dark, whether red or blue.
Final night, in whose depth one feels
the roots' voice, altitude's breath.

I push ahead under your skin, and distance is blood.
My body pushes through in a thick constellation.
The universe crowds together its errant echoes,
there where the history of humanity is written.

Looking at, seeing round the solitude, the mountain,
the sea, through the window of an entire heart,
which grieved yesterday at not being a horizon
open to a world less mutable and transient.

Acumular la piedra y el niño para nada.
Para vivir sin alas y oscuramente un día.
Pirámide de sal temible y limitada
sin fuego ni frescura. No. Vuelve, vida mía.

Mas algo me ha empujado desesperadamente.
Caigo en la madrugada del tiempo, del pasado.
Me arrojan de la noche ante la luz hiriente.
Vuelvo a llorar desnudo, pequeño, regresado.

A stone and a child grow for nothing.
To live darkly, without wings, for a day.
Terrible circumscribed pyramid of salt,
with neither fire nor coolness. No. Go back, life.

Yet something has shoved me desperately ahead.
I tumble through the dawn of time, and the past.
I am thrown from night into the stinging light,
I am crying again—tiny, regressed.

DON SHARE

133

El hombre no reposa: quien reposa es su traje
cuando, colgado, mece su soledad con viento.
Mas, una vida incógnita como un vago tatuaje
mueve bajo las ropas dejadas un aliento.

El corazón ya cesa de ser flor de oleaje.
La frente ya no rige su potro, el firmamento.
Por más que el cuerpo, ahondando por quietud, trabaje,
En el centro reposo se cierne el movimiento.

No hay muertos. Todo vive: todo late y avanza.
Todo es un soplo extático de actividad moviente.
Piel inferior del hombre, su traje no ha expirado.

Visiblemente inmóvil, el corazón se lanza
A conmover al mundo que recorrió la frente.
Y el universo gira como un pecho pausado.

THE MAN DOES NOT REST . . .

The man does not rest: what rests is his suit
when, hung, it rocks lonely in the wind.
But a hidden life like a vague tattoo
moves under those lazy clothes, breathing in.

The heart has already ceased to be a swelling flower.
The mind no longer governs its colt, the firmament.
No matter how hard the body, sinking into quiet, works,
in the center rests, blossoming, a movement.

There are no dead. Everything lives: it throbs and surges.
Everything is an ecstatic whirl of exciting designs.
Man's skin is inferior, but his suit does not rest.

Though stone-still to the eye, the heart is sent to stir
the world that traveled across the mind.
And the universe expands like a slow chest.

[SIGO EN LA SOMBRA, LLENO DE LUZ]

Sigo en la sombra, lleno de luz: ¿existe el día?
¿Esto es mi tumba o es mi bóveda materna?
Pasa el latido contra mi piel como una fría
loza que germina caliente, roja, tierna.

Es posible que no haya nacido todavía,
o que haya muerto siempre. La sombra me gobierna.
Si esto es vivir, morir no sé yo qué sería,
ni sé lo que persigo con ansia tan eterna.

Encadenado a un traje, parece que persigo
desnundarme, librarme de aquello que no puede
ser yo y hace turbia y ausente la mirada.

Pero la tela negra, distante, va conmigo
sombra con sombra, contra la sombra hasta que ruede
a la desnuda vida creciente de la nada.

[I LIVE IN SHADOW, FILLED WITH LIGHT]

I live in shadow, filled with light. Does day
exist? Is this grave or mother's womb?
Against my skin a throbbing makes its way
like frozen stone sprouting red, tender, warm.

Maybe I'm waiting to be born or see
that I've been always dead. These shadows rule
me, and if living's this, what can death be?
Intensely groping and the eternal fool,

chained to my clothes, it looks like I go on
stripping and getting rid of everything,
leaving me gone, my eyes in far distress.

But the remote black clothing that I don
plods with me: shadows, shadows, shadows fling
me through bare life growing from nothingness.

WILLIS BARNSTONE

SEPULTURA DE LA IMAGINACIÓN

Un albañil quería. . . . No le faltaba aliento.
Un albañil quería, piedra tras piedra, muro
tras muro, levantar una imagen al viento
desencadenador en el futuro.

Quería un edificio capaz de lo más leve.
No le faltaba aliento. ¡Cuánto aquel ser quería!
Piedras de plumas, muros de pájaros los mueve
una imaginación al mediodía.

Reía. Trabajaba. Cantaba. De sus brazos,
con un poder más alto que el ala de los truenos,
iban brotando muros lo mismo que aletazos.
Pero los aletazos duran menos.

Al fin, era la piedra su agente. Y la montaña
tiene valor de vuelo si es totalmente activa.
Piedra por piedra es peso y hunde cuanto acompaña
aunque esto sea un mundo de ansia viva.

Un albañil quería. . . . Pero la piedra cobra
su torva densidad brutal en un momento.
Aquel hombre labraba su cárcel. Y en su obra
fueron precipitados él y el viento.

IMAGINATION'S TOMB

A mason wanted. . . . He wasn't lacking spirit.
A mason wanted, stone by stone, wall
by wall, to erect a monument to the wind,
that unchainer of the future.

He wanted a structure capable of delicate things.
He wasn't lacking spirit. How much he wanted it!
At midday the imagination moves stones
like feathers, walls like birds.

He laughed. Worked. Sang. From his arms,
more powerful than thunder's wings,
walls flew out like wingbeats.
But wingbeats don't last like this.

At last, stone was his medium. And a mountain
when it moves is able to fly, but stone by stone,
it grows heavy and crushes all that it escorts
even a world alive with desire.

A mason wanted. . . . But stone exacts
its strict brutal thickness in a second.
That man was building his prison. And into it
the mason and the wind were flung.

TED GENOWAYS

ETERNA SOMBRA

Yo que creí que la luz era mía
precipitado en la sombra me veo.
Ascua solar, sideral alegría
ígnea de espuma, de luz, de deseo.

Sangre ligera, redonda, granada:
raudo anhelar sin perfil ni penumbra.
Fuera, la luz en la luz sepultada.
Siento que sólo la sombra me alumbra.

Sólo la sombra. Sin astro. Sin cielo.
Seres. Volúmenes. Cuerpos tangibles
dentro del aire que no tiene vuelo,
dentro del árbol de los imposibles.

Cárdenos ceños, pasiones de luto.
Dientes sedientos de ser colorados.
Oscuridad de rencor absoluto.
Cuerpos lo mismo que pozos cegados.

Falta el espacio. Se ha hundido la risa.
Ya no es posible lanzarse a la altura.
El corazón quiere ser más de prisa
fuerza que ensancha la estrecha negrura.

Carne sin norte que va en oleada
hacia la noche siniestra, baldía.
¿Quién es el rayo de sol que la invada?
Busco. No encuentro ni rastro del día.

Sólo el fulgor de los puños cerrados,
el resplandor de los dientes que acechan.
Dientes y puños de todos los lados.
Más que las manos, los montes se estrechan.

ETERNAL DARKNESS

I who was sure the light was mine
see myself thrown down into darkness.
Sun-like cinder, star-like joy,
fiery with sea foam, with light and desire.

Blood that is light, circular, erect:
rough longing with no outline or shadow.
Outside, the light buried inside the light.
I feel only the darkness makes me luminous.

Only the darkness. Without a star. Without sky.
Shapes. Beings. Material bodies
inside the air that is without wings,
inside the tree trunk of impossible things.

Pale frowns, the passions dressed in black.
Teeth that are longing to be red.
The shadowiness of pure revenge.
Bodies that resemble plugged wells.

Too little room. Laughter has gone under.
To fly up to high places is impossible.
The heart wants quickly to become
what breaks open the narrow blackness.

Unguided body that goes like a big wave
toward the night that is ominous and barren.
Who is the ray of sun that storms into it?
I look around. Not a trace of daylight.

Only the light reflected from closed fists,
from luminous teeth on the march.
Everywhere I look, fists and teeth.
More than hands, mountains reach out to us.

Turbia es la lucha sin sed de mañana.
¡Qué lejanía de opacos latidos!
Soy una cárcel con una ventana
ante una gran soledad de rugidos.

Soy una abierta ventana que escucha,
por donde va tenebrosa la vida.
Pero hay un rayo de sol en la lucha
que siempre deja la sombra vencida.

A fight without thirst for the future is nothing.
What a vast plain of dark heartbeats!
I'm a prison cell with one window,
looking out on a huge solitude of barks.

I'm an open window that listens,
where life goes by, full of shadows.
But fighting there is one ray of sunlight
always that leaves the darkness beaten.

TIMOTHY BALAND AND ROBERT BLY

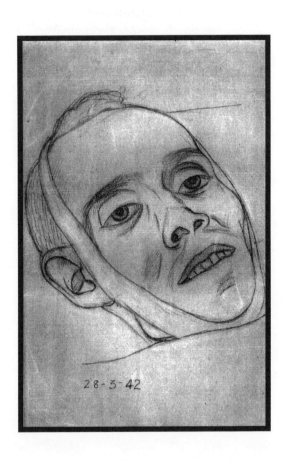

28-3-42

The Funeral and Burial

They couldn't make his eyes stay closed. Though Miguel Hernández's death certificate lists cause of death as "hyperthyroidism"—thus explaining his widely dilated pupils—the real cause was advanced tuberculosis. To this day, no further explanation has been officially made, apart from the chilling popular wisdom about the Fascist prisons: *Cuando entré en la cárcel ya estaba en el ataúd*—"He who enters the prison is already in the coffin."[1] The body was scheduled to be turned over to the family later that day.

Hernández's older brother Vicente immediately set about arranging a "proper burial." Though he had repeatedly insisted on a grave burial, the poet who once proclaimed "Clay is my profession and my destiny" would be interred in a sepulchre. Vicente later remembered: "All day, with Justino Marín, brother of Ramón Sijé, who accompanied me, we spent taking measures so that he would not be buried in the earth, like a pauper, but in a niche."[2]

Meanwhile, Hernández's friends petitioned the prison directors for permission to cast a death mask. That request denied, an artist was allowed inside to prepare a drawing, then the body was removed from the infirmary.

That afternoon, his fellow inmates were allowed to hold a small ceremony. They gathered on the interior patio. The makeshift prison band played a funeral march and the coffin, draped in the Loyalist flag of Spain, was carried on the shoulders of four inmates. The coffin was lowered and slid through a small door in the prison wall, where the funeral coach waited. The funeral processional formed: his widow Josefina, Gabriel Sijé, Ricardo Fuente and Miguel Abad Miró, Hernández's brother Vicente, his sister Elvira, and his other sister's husband Ismael Tares.[3] The processional, led by a train of horses, without a single wreath, moved down the Madrid road until they turned right at the

1. Bravo Morata, 264.
2. Quoted in Nichols, 129.
3. Guerrero Zamora, 189.

Nuestra Señora del Remedio cemetery. It was six o'clock, near dusk and cloudy. A light wind rippled the dresses of the veiled women. Abad Miró opened the box—of plain, unfinished wood—to identify Miguel Hernández. At first, he did not recognize his friend. He looked like "a doll from the fair"[4]—compact, shrunken, a skull and two open eyes. Miró tried again, unsuccessfully, to close Hernández's eyes. Josefina was overcome by grief and threw herself across the body, kissing it desperately.

The body was interred in niche 1009, group 68, row 1. Belda, the friend who had paid for the niche, went the following day to visit Hernández's father, who still had received no word of Miguel's death. Upon arriving at the home of the long-estranged father, Belda asked:
    —Do you know about Miguel?

Hernández's father responded in turn with another question:
    —Has he died?
    —Yes.
    —Then he has found what he was looking for.[5]

4. Zardoya, 49.
5. Bravo Morata, 265–266.

RECOGED ESA VOZ

POR OCTAVIO PAZ

En una cárcel de su pueblo natal, Orihuela, ha muerto Miguel Hernández. Ha muerto solo, en una España hostil, enemiga de la España en que vivió su juventud, adversaria de la España que soñó su generosidad. Que otros maldigan a sus victimarios; que otros analicen y estudien su poesía. Yo quiero recordarlo.

Lo conocí cantando canciones populares españolas, en 1937. Poseía voz de bajo, un poco cerril, un poco de animal inocente: sonaba a campo, a eco grave repetido por los valles, a piedra cayendo en un barranco. Tenía ojos oscuros de avellana, limpios, sin nada retorcido o intelectual; la boca, como las manos y el corazón, era grande y, como ellos, simple y jugosa, hecha de barro por unas manos puras y torpes; de mediana estatura, más bien robusto, era ágil, con la agilidad reposada de la sangre y los musculos, con la gravedad ágil de lo terrestre: se veía que era más próximo de los potros serios y de los novillos melancólicos que de aquellos atormentados intelectuales compañeros suyos; llevaba la cabeza casi rapada y usaba pantalones de pana y alpargatas: parecía un soldado o un campesino. En aquella sala de un hotel de Valencia, llena de humo, de vanidad y, también, de pasión verdadera, Miguel Hernández cantaba con su voz de bajo y su cantar era como si todos los árboles cantaran Como si un solo árbol, el árbol de una España naciente y milenaria, empezara a cantar de nuevo sus canciones. Ni chopo, ni olivo, ni encina, ni manzano, ni naranjo, sino todos ellos juntos, fundidas sus savias, sus aromas y sus hojas en ese árbol de carne y voz. Imposible recordarlo con palabras; más que en la memoria, "en el sabor del tiempo queda escrito".

Después le oí recitar poemas de amor y de guerra. A través de los versos—y no sabría decfr ahora cómo eran o qué decían esos versos—, como a través de una cortina de luz lujosa, se oía mugir y gemir, se oía agonizar a un animal tierno y poderoso, un toro quizá, muerto en la tarde, alzando los ojos asombrados hacia unos impasibles espectadores de humo. Y ya no quisiera recordarlo más, ahora que tanto lo recuerdo. Sé que fuimos amigos; que caminamos por Madrid en ruinas y por Valencia, de noche, junto al mar, o por callejuelas intrincadas; sé que le gustaba trepar a los árboles y comer sandias, en tabernas de soldados; sé que después lo vi en París y que su presencia fue como una ráfaga de sol, de pan, en la ciudad negra. Lo recuerdo todo, pero no quisiera recor-

BY OCTAVIO PAZ

In a prison in the village of his birth, Orihuela, Miguel Hernández died. He died alone, in a hostile Spain, enemy of the Spain where he lived out his youth, adversary of the Spain that rang with his generosity. Let others curse his torturers; let others analyze and study his poetry. I want to remember *him*.

I first encountered him singing songs of the Spanish people, in 1937. He spoke in a low voice, a bit untrained, a bit like an innocent animal: sounding like the countryside, like a deep echo repeating through the valleys, like a stone falling from a cliff. He had dark eyes, hazel and clear, not twisted or intellectual; his mouth, like his hands and his heart, was large and, like them, simple and fleshy, made of mud by pure and clumsy hands; of average height, sort of robust, he was agile, with agility born of the blood and the muscles, with the agile gravity of the earthly: one could see he was more akin to the somber colts and the melancholy bullocks than his tormented intellectual companions; he kept his head almost shaved and wore corduroy pants and espadrilles: he looked like a soldier or a farmer. In the lobby of that hotel in Valencia, full of smoke, of vanity and, also, of rightful passion, Miguel Hernández sang with his deep voice and his singing was as if all the trees were singing. It was as if one tree, the tree of a nascent and millenary Spain, were beginning to sing its songs anew. Not the poplar, not the olive tree, nor the oak, not the apple, nor the orange, but all of those together, fusing their saps, their smells and their leaves in this tree of flesh and voice. It is impossible to remember him in words; more than in memory, "in the flavor of time he is written."

Later I heard him recite poems of love and war. Through verses—and I cannot say now how they were or what those verses said[6]—as if through a curtain of luxurious light, one could hear a moaning or lowing, one could hear the death throes of a tender and powerful animal, a bull perhaps, dying in the afternoon, raising its eyes astonished toward the passive, ghost-like spectators. And now I don't want to remember him anymore, now that I remember him so well. I know that we were

6. Hernández's war poems had been banned in Spain and thus were largely unavailable at the time Paz composed this essay.

darlo . . . No quiero recordarte, Miguel, gran amigo de unos pocos diás milagrosos y fuera del tiempo, días de pasión en los que, al descubrirte, al descubrir a España, descubrí una parte de mí, una raíz áspera y tierna, que me hizo más grande y más antiguo. Que otros te recuerden. Déjame que te olvide, porque el olvido de lo puro y de lo verdadero, el olvido de lo mejor, nos da fuerzas para seguir viviendo en este mundo de compromisos y reverencias, de saludos y ceremonias, maloliente y podrido. Déjame que te olvide, para que en este olvido siga creciendo tu voz, hurtada ya a tu cuerpo y a la memoria de los que te conocimos, libre y alta en los aires, desasida del tiempo y de su miseria.

MÉXICO, 1942

friends; that we walked amid the ruins of Madrid and of Valencia, at night, near the sea, or the intricate side streets; I know that he liked to climb trees and eat watermelon, in taverns frequented by soldiers; I know that later I saw him in Paris and that his presence was like a ray of sunlight, a shock of wheat, in the black city. I remember everything, but I don't want to remember . . . I don't want to remember you, Miguel, great friend of so few days, miraculous and outside of time, days of passion, when I discovered you, as I discovered Spain, and I discovered a part of myself, a rough and tender root, that made me both larger and more ancient. Let others remember you. Let me forget you, because forgetting is pure and true, forgetting our good times gives us the strength to continue living in this world of compromises and reverences, of salutes and ceremonies, fetid and rotting. Let me forget you, so that in this forgetting your voice can continue to grow, stolen now from your body and in the memory of those of us who knew you, free and tall on the wind, unchained from time and from your misery.

MEXICO, 1942

TED GENOWAYS

3 [The Bull] (page 23)

This poem is spoken in the voice of the bull challenging the matadors to come to the ring. As Sánchez Vidal points out, the lyric progression is built on an elaborate series of puns and metaphors centering on the horns of the bull (Hernández, *Perito en lunas/El rayo que no cesa*, 87). The horns form the bow through which the body of the bull is fired. Later, they transform into the hooks of an anchor and the upward curve of a mustache. There are also more veiled evocations of the hooked horns in the less-than-quarter moon and the semicircle of a sand-gulf. In the original Spanish, both of these images are further complicated by puns. *La hora es de mi luna menos cuarto* literally can be read as either "It is a quarter before the hour of my moon" or "It is the hour of my less-than-quarter moon." Even more elaborate, the inserted phrase *golfo de arena* in the final line can be read literally as "sand-gulf" or figuratively as "the gulf [i.e. sand floor] of the [bullfighting] arena." Typical of Hernández's early flights of fancy, the use of the anchor as a metaphor is supported by the imagery of a gulf, but the metaphor of the mustache is unexpected and not reinforced by other images in the poem.

4 [The Bullfighter] (page 25)

Spoken in the voice of a matador, this octava responds directly to the previous poem spoken by the bull. The opening is fairly straightforward until the phrase *de liras el alma te corona*. This can be interpreted as "the soul crowns you with lyric poetry" or more literally "the soul crowns you with lyres." The first meaning suggests the poet's own exultation of bulls as the national symbol of Spain; the second reading, however, creates the visual parallel of the horns of the bull and the inverted arc of the Greek lyre. In order to evoke both, I have translated the line as "[the soul] crowns you with lyres and poetry." The final image of the poem is also complex. The bull's anger draws it toward the center of the ring. Viewed aerially, the ring would appear to be a wheel. (The same pun on *arena* as both "sand" and "stadium" is employed here as in the previous poem.) The crowd yells derisively at the bull even as the stands become part of the wheel spinning around the axis of the bullfight.

35 [Oven and Moon] (page 29)

The oven, in this poem, is represented as *un constante estío de ceniza* ("an unending summer of ash"). The moon, when placed inside the oven, is likened to a loaf of bread, made from the threshing floor and baked until it is golden. Sánchez Vidal has postulated that the "impossible" moon represents Hernández's desire to become a poet, while the bread moon that lies "within reach" symbolizes his humble life in Orihuela (Hernández, *Perito en lunas/El rayo que no cesa*, 132–133). In any case, the poet is left considering whether the poetic moon or the earthly moon is superior.

36 [Undertaker and Cemetery] (page 31)

The opening four lines address the undertaker directly, while the final four lines are a circuitous description of a cemetery. These lines are some of the most significant in *Perito en lunas,* primarily because they are revisited in a major poem, "Vecino de la muerte" ("Death's Neighbor"), composed in 1936. The opening line of that poem (*Patio de vecindad que nadie alquila*/ Neighborhood patio that nobody rents) is recycled almost directly from this octava. The line carries the double meaning of being forever followed by death, and thus a "neighbor" to death, and being literally laid to rest next to the "neighboring" dead in a cemetery. The full implications of this marriage to death both in life and after life are only glossed in this poem, but are explored much more fully three years later.

15 [I call myself clay though Miguel is my name] (page 67)

Richard Seybolt, taking his cue from Allen Tate's assertion that "we can have multiple meaning through ambiguity, but we cannot have an incoherent structure of images," analyzes the "ordered chaos" of this poem with remarkable insight. He concludes, again drawing on Tate's notions of "intension and extension," that Hernández "consciously reunites in an exact way these two elements, creating a processed poem of profound poetic emotion." For his meticulous study of the complex structure of this poem, see Richard A. Seybolt's "Caos ordenado: 'Me llamo barro aunque Miguel me llame,'" *Explicacion de Textos Literarios* 9 (1980–1981): 3–13; Allen Tate, "Tension in Poetry," in *On the Limits of Poetry* (New York: Swallow Press, 1948), 82.

29 Elegy (page 97)

Ana M. Fagundo writes of this poem, "Form and function (emotion and expression) have to operate in harmony to produce this miracle we call a poem. I believe that there will be no danger in asserting that the elegy for Ramón Sijé is one of the most beautiful and fully realized poems by Miguel Hernández." For her full study of the rhetoric of this poem, see "Emotividad y expresión en la 'Elegía' a Ramón Sijé," *Romance Notes* 11 (1969): 256–260. For a more biographical and personal reading, see Jose Muñoz Garrigos's "El último episodio de la amistad entre Miguel Hernández y Ramón Sijé: 'La elegia,'" *Insula: Revista de letras y ciencias humanas* 47.544 (April 1992): 3–4.

First Elegy (page 157)

Salvatore J. Poeta writes of the elegy for Lorca: "In comparison with the tender friendship that he initiated and maintained with the grand intellect and devout Christian Ramón Sijé, before his death, Miguel Hernández had barely gotten to know Federico García Lorca. The friendship with the poet from Granada was reduced to little more than the correspondence over Hernández's *Expert in Moons.* For this reason, there seems no competition between the two great funeral elegies, between the emotional intensity and the wild rage that they caused in the spirit of the Shepherd of Orihuela." For his in-depth analysis of the poem see "Elegia de Miguel Hernández en memoria de Federico García Lorca analizada," *Hispanic Journal* 6.2 (Spring 1985): 173–183.

Winds of the People (page 171)

For the best English-language interpretation of this poem see Marilyn Rosenthal, *Poetry of the Spanish Civil War* (New York: NYU Press, 1975): 45–48.

Gather This Voice (page 183)

For a detailed interpretation of this poem see Marilyn Rosenthal, *Poetry of the Spanish Civil War* (New York: NYU Press, 1975): 53–58.

Worthy of Being a Commander, line 24 (page 205)

Lt. Valentín González, popularly known as El Campesino (which literally means "peasant" or "farmer"), was the leader of the Loyalist army.

Memorial to the 5th Regiment, line 14 (page 213)

The line *como un río de leones* is an allusion to Lorca's "Llanto por Ignacio Sánchez Mejías" ("Lament for Ignacio Sánchez Mejías"), which contains the lines:

> No hubo príncipe en Sevilla
> que comparársele pueda,
> ni espada como su espada
> ni corazón tan de veras.
> Como un río de leones
> su maravillosa fuerza,
> y como un torso de mármol
> su dibujada prudencia.
>
> . . . . . .
>
> There was no prince in Seville
> who could compare to him,
> nor any sword like his sword
> nor any heart so true.
> Like a river of lions
> his marvelous force,
> and like a marble bust
> his chiseled prudence.

Lorca's poem was first published in 1935 and would have been fresh in Hernández's mind.

9 Waltz Poem of Those in Love and Inseparable Forever (page 285)

Manuscript drafts of this poem indicate that it was composed in 1938. However, in the last part of 1939, Hernández transcribed the poem into the notebook of a friend. Thus earlier editions of this poem carried the note "(Escrita en la Prisión de Conde de Toreno, a fines de 1939, para el álbun de un amigo)," which Timothy Baland translates as "(Written in Count of Tore Prison at the end of 1939, in the album of a friend.)" It is that version from which the title is drawn.

12 [The sun, the rose, and the child] (page 289)

An earlier version of this poem had a third stanza that read:

> Vivo lo que vivo hoy,
> lo que estoy soñando es nuestro,
> hacia atrás, hacia adelante

por las orillas del cuerpo.

. . . . . .

I live what I live today,
what I am dreaming is ours,
backward, forward
by the borders of the body.

49 [The aged in the villages] (page 305)

For an analysis of this poem, see James Whiston's "La inversion de la retorica en 'La vejez en los pueblos' de Miguel Hernández," in *Miguel Hernández, cincuenta años despues,* ed. Jose Carlos Rovira (Alicante: Comision de Homenaje a Miguel Hernández, 1993): 983–986.

62 from *The Rain* (page 325)

This excerpt was prepared by Timothy Baland in the 1960s. At the time, this was the only version of this poem available in any language. Sánchez Vidal has since uncovered a longer version of the poem; this later draft, however, is unfinished and fragmentary. Thus, the abbreviated and familiar version is offered in its place.

64 Before Hatred (page 327)

Carlos Bousoño points to this poem as the beginning of "the 'new' generation of 'autobiographical poetry'" in Spain. He writes: "The piece expresses a determined human situation for the poet, and he writes with emotional accents from his personal life. We feel in each word that this is not the disembodied voice of a purely literary protagonist, but rather the trembling and the spiritual movements of a man named Miguel, situated in a concrete and pathetic circumstance of post-war Spain." See Bousoño's "Notas sobre un poema de Miguel: 'Antes del odio,'" in Ifach's *Miguel Hernández.*

79 Lullabies of the Onion (page 351)

Perhaps Hernández's best known poem and generally considered among his finest, "Lullabies of the Onion" was, in fact, intended to be untitled, like all the other poems in *Cancionero.* In 1946, when the poem was originally published in the Spanish literary magazine *Halcón (The Falcon),* it bore the title "Nana a mi niño" ("Lullaby to My Son"). The title "Lullabies of the Onion," however, became so firmly attached to the poem that the editors of *Obra completa* decided to leave it in place; I have followed that decision. Early published versions also carried a brief note explaining the biographical origin of the poem: "Dedicadas a su hijo, a raíz de recibir una carta de su mujer, en la que decía que no comía más que pan y cebolla," which Levine translates, "Dedicated to his son, after receiving a letter from his wife saying that all she had to eat was bread and onion." For Levine's own analysis of this poem, see the *Kenyon Review* 11.4 (Fall 1989): 145–159. See also Luis Felipe Vivanco's "Las nanas de la cebolla" in *En torno a Miguel Hernández,* ed. Juan Cano Ballesta (Madrid: Castalia, 1978): 136–141.

117 The Last Corner (page 357)

For a biographical and technical analysis of this poem, see Marina Mayoral, "'El ultimó rincón' de Miguel Hernández," in *En torno a Miguel Hernández,* ed. Juan Cano Ballesta (Madrid: Castalia, 1978): 95–108.

122 Lament of the Thirsting Man (page 367)

See Francis Cerdan, "Lectura de la Casida del sediento de Miguel Hernández," in *Miguel Hernández, cincuenta anos despues,* ed. Jose Carlos Rovira (Alicante: Comision de Homenaje a Miguel Hernández, 1993): 983–986.

Barnstone, Willis, trans. *Six Masters of the Spanish Sonnet.* Carbondale: Southern Illinois University Press, 1993.

Benardete, M. J., and Rolfe Humphries, eds. . . . *and Spain Sings: Fifty Loyalist Ballads Adapted by American Poets.* New York: Vanguard Press, 1937.

Bravo Morata, Federico. *Miguel Hernández.* Madrid: Fenicia, 1979.

Cano Ballesta, Juan. *La poesía de Miguel Hernández.* 2nd ed. Madrid: Editorial Gredos, 1971.

Fonseca Fernández, Guillermo. "A Miguel Hernández." *Litoral* 73–75 (Spring 1978): 183–185.

Gibson, Ian. *The Assassination of Federico García Lorca.* New York: Penguin Books, 1983.

Guerrero Zamora, Juan. *Miguel Hernández, Poeta (1910–1942).* Madrid: El Grifon, 1955.

Hernández, Miguel. *Obra Completa,* Agustín Sánchez Vidal and José Carlos Rovira, eds., in collaboration with Carmen Alemany. Madrid: Espasa-Calpe, 1992.

———. *Poesía y prosa de guerra y otros textos olvidados.* Juan Cano Ballesta and Robert Marrast, eds. Madrid: Editorial Ayusa, 1977.

———. *Perito en lunas/El rayo que no cesa.* Agustín Sánchez Vidal, ed. Madrid: Alhambra, 1976.

Hernández, Miguel, and Blas de Otero. *Selected Poems.* Timothy Baland and Hardie St. Martin, eds. Boston: Beacon Press, 1972.

Ifach, María de Gracia, ed. *Miguel Hernández.* Madrid: Taurus, 1975.

Neruda, Pablo. *Memoirs.* Hardie St. Martin, trans. New York: Farrar, Straus and Giroux, 1977.

Nichols, Geraldine Cleary. *Miguel Hernández.* Boston: Twayne Publishers, 1978.

Paz, Octavio. *Primeras letras, 1931–1943.* Enrico Mario Santí, ed. México, D. F.: Vuelta, 1988.

Schwartz, Kessel, ed. *Introduction to Modern Spanish Literature.* New York: Twayne Publishers, 1968.

Spender, Stephen, and John Lehmann, eds. *Poems for Spain.* London: Hogarth Press, 1939.

Williams, William Carlos. *The Collected Poems of William Carlos Williams,* vol. 1, *1909–1939.* A. Walton Litz and Christopher MacGowan, eds. New York: New Directions, 1986.

Zardoya, Concha. *Miguel Hernández, vida y obra.* New York: Hispanic Institute in the United States, 1955.

TIMOTHY BALAND edited the Hernández portion of *Miguel Hernández and Blas de Otero: Selected Poems.* This work forms the cornerstone of translations of Miguel Hernández into English. Baland is now a judge living in central Minnesota.

WILLIS BARNSTONE is Distinguished Professor of Comparative Literature, Spanish, and East Asian Cultures at Indiana University. He has written more than forty books of poetry, scholarship, translation, and memoir, including *Sunday Morning in Fascist Spain: A European Memoir* (1995), *With Borges on an Ordinary Evening in Buenos Aires* (1993), *The Poetics of Translation* (1993), *The Other Bible* (1984), and two books of poems nominated for the Pulitzer Prize, *China Poems* (1972) and *From This White Island* (1959). Among his most recent translations is *Six Masters of the Spanish Sonnet* (1996), which includes a number of poems by Miguel Hernández.

ROBERT BLY, though best known as a poet and essayist, is one of our most significant translators. From Spanish alone, he has translated Pablo Neruda, Antonio Machado, César Vallejo, Juan Ramón Jiménez, Vicente Aleixandre, and Miguel Hernández. In 1968, he dedicated a special issue of his literary magazine, *The Sixties,* to the material that would eventually comprise the Hernández portion of *Miguel Hernández and Blas de Otero: Selected Poems* (1972), edited by Timothy Baland and Hardie St. Martin.

TED GENOWAYS has published his translations of Miguel Hernández in *Partisan Review, Quarterly West,* and *Virginia Quarterly Review.* A specialist in conflict literature, he is also coeditor of *A Perfect Picture of Hell: Eyewitness Accounts by Civil War Prisoners from the 12th Iowa* (2001), and author of *Bullroarer* (2001), a collection of poems selected for the Samuel French Morse Poetry Prize by Marilyn Hacker.

JOHN HAINES'S most recent books are *Living Off the Country: Essays on Poetry and Place* (1999) and *Fables and Distances: New and Selected Essays* (1996). He is a widely respected poet and essayist.

GEOFFREY HOLIDAY, until his untimely death in August 2000, was a distinguished Spanish translator who lived in South Africa. In addition to his translations of Miguel Hernández, Holiday wrote a biography of Hernández, entitled *The Wind and the Harvest.* He also published translations of Juan Ramón Jiménez and translated the whole of Vicente Aleixandre's *Destruccion o amor.*

EDWIN HONIG is a distinguished poet and translator. He established himself as an authority on Spanish poetry with *Federico García Lorca* (1944), the first significant volume of the poet available in English. Since then he has translated dozens of books from Spanish and Portuguese, most recently *Poems of Fernando*

Pessoa (1998), and written about the craft of translation, including the book *The Poet's Other Voice: Conversations on Literary Translation* (1985). In 1989, he published *The Unending Lightning: The Selected Poems of Miguel Hernández.*

PHILIP LEVINE has received a Pulitzer Prize and two National Book Awards for his own poetry. His books of Spanish translations include *Off the Map: Selected Poems of Gloria Fuerte* (1984) and *Tarumba: The Selected Poems of Jaime Sabines* (1976).

GARY J. SCHMECHEL is a translator living in Seattle, Washington. He has translated the entirety of Miguel Hernández's collection *El cancionero y romancero de ausencias.*

DON SHARE is a poet and translator from Spanish and classical languages. His books include *Seneca in English* (1998) and *I Have Lots of Heart: Selected Poems of Miguel Hernández* (1997), which received the 1999 Times Literary Supplement Award for translation. He is the poetry editor of *Partisan Review.*

JAMES WRIGHT won the Pulitzer Prize for his *Collected Poems and Translations* (1971). His Spanish translations included poems by Pablo Neruda, Juan Ramón Jiménez, Jorge Guillén, César Vallejo, Pedro Salinas, and Miguel Hernández.